INTERNATIONAL DEVELOPMENT IN FOCUS

Maritime Networks, Port Efficiency, and Hinterland Connectivity in the Mediterranean

Jean-François Arvis, Vincent Vesin,
Robin Carruthers, César Ducruet, and
Peter de Langen

© 2019 International Bank for Reconstruction and Development / The World Bank
1818 H Street NW, Washington, DC 20433
Telephone: 202-473-1000; Internet: www.worldbank.org

Some rights reserved

1 2 3 4   22 21 20 19

Books in this series are published to communicate the results of Bank research, analysis, and operational experience with the least possible delay. The extent of language editing varies from book to book.

This work is a product of the staff of The World Bank with external contributions. The findings, interpretations, and conclusions expressed in this work do not necessarily reflect the views of The World Bank, its Board of Executive Directors, or the governments they represent. The World Bank does not guarantee the accuracy of the data included in this work. The boundaries, colors, denominations, and other information shown on any map in this work do not imply any judgment on the part of The World Bank concerning the legal status of any territory or the endorsement or acceptance of such boundaries.

Nothing herein shall constitute or be considered to be a limitation upon or waiver of the privileges and immunities of The World Bank, all of which are specifically reserved.

Rights and Permissions

This work is available under the Creative Commons Attribution 3.0 IGO license (CC BY 3.0 IGO) http://creativecommons.org/licenses/by/3.0/igo. Under the Creative Commons Attribution license, you are free to copy, distribute, transmit, and adapt this work, including for commercial purposes, under the following conditions:

Attribution—Please cite the work as follows: Arvis, Jean-François, Vincent Vesin, Robin Carruthers, César Ducruet, and Peter de Langen. 2019. *Maritime Networks, Port Efficiency, and Hinterland Connectivity in the Mediterranean.* International Development in Focus. Washington, DC: World Bank. doi:10.1596/978-1-4648-1274-3 License: Creative Commons Attribution CC BY 3.0 IGO

Translations—If you create a translation of this work, please add the following disclaimer along with the attribution: *This translation was not created by The World Bank and should not be considered an official World Bank translation. The World Bank shall not be liable for any content or error in this translation.*

Adaptations—If you create an adaptation of this work, please add the following disclaimer along with the attribution: *This is an adaptation of an original work by The World Bank. Views and opinions expressed in the adaptation are the sole responsibility of the author or authors of the adaptation and are not endorsed by The World Bank.*

Third-party content—The World Bank does not necessarily own each component of the content contained within the work. The World Bank therefore does not warrant that the use of any third-party-owned individual component or part contained in the work will not infringe on the rights of those third parties. The risk of claims resulting from such infringement rests solely with you. If you wish to re-use a component of the work, it is your responsibility to determine whether permission is needed for that re-use and to obtain permission from the copyright owner. Examples of components can include, but are not limited to, tables, figures, or images.

All queries on rights and licenses should be addressed to World Bank Publications, The World Bank Group, 1818 H Street NW, Washington, DC 20433, USA; e-mail: pubrights@worldbank.org.

ISBN: 978-1-4648-1274-3
DOI: 10.1596/978-1-4648-1274-3

Cover photo: © Tanger Med. Used with the permission of Tanger Med. Permission required for reuse.
Cover design: Debra Naylor / Naylor Design Inc.

Contents

Foreword vii
Preface ix
Acknowledgments xiii
About the Authors/Editors xv
Executive Summary xvii
Abbreviations xxvii

CHAPTER 1: Dimensions, Indicators, and Drivers of Trade Connectivity in the Mediterranean 1
    The Mediterranean: The nexus of world trade or its own small world? 1
    Trade connectivity and economic development 4
    Measuring trade connectivity: Indicators 7
    Using indicators to measure performance of the main Mediterranean ports 10
    Drivers of trade connectivity 12
    Connectivity patterns 13
    Annex 1A: Potential indicators at the country and port levels 14
    Notes 16
    References 17

CHAPTER 2: Maritime Networks and Port Efficiency 19
    The global connectivity of Mediterranean ports 19
    Local connectivity of Mediterranean ports 25
    A typology of Mediterranean ports by maritime networks and port efficiency 36
    Annex 2A: Data and methodology 38
    Annex 2B: Explanation of network measures 40
    Annex 2C: Top 20 Mediterranean ports by traffic performance and network centrality scores 40
    Notes 45
    References 45

CHAPTER 3: Hinterland Connectivity 47
    Indicators of hinterland connectivity 47
    Annex 3A: Identifying a port's hinterland 60
    Characteristics of port hinterlands 60
    Notes 66
    References 67

CHAPTER 4: Three Case Studies on the Connectivity of Ports 69
  Port market shares in Spain 69
  Port Said East (Egypt) 72
  Tanger Med (Morocco) 75
  Annex 4A: Port choice: Statistical analysis of Spain 78
  Data 78
  Notes 83
  References 84

CHAPTER 5: Enhancing Connectivity and Port Development Strategies 85
  Port development strategy and hinterland dynamic 85
  A typology of ports by connectivity and development strategy 87
  Patterns of port development and evolutionary strategies in the Mediterranean 88
  Notes 91
  References 92

Appendix A: Guide to Port Locations 93

Appendix B: Descriptions of 17 Major Mediterranean Ports 95

Glossary 105

Boxes
1.1 The liner shipping connectivity index 7
1.2 The logistics performance index 8
3.1 The size of a port's hinterland 48
3A.1 Identifying port hinterlands in Morocco 64

Figures
ES.1 Three dimensions of trade connectivity xviii
ES.2 Three port development paths and strategies xxii
ES.3 Typology of port connectivity xxiii
1.1 Three dimensions of trade connectivity 6
B1.1.1 Liner shipping connectivity index values for major hubs and gateways, 2004–16 8
B1.2.1 Logistics performance index values for selected countries, 2007–16 9
1.2 Breakdown of modes in total short-sea shipping traffic in European regions, 2015 11
2.1 Extra-Mediterranean traffic of Mediterranean ports, by region, 2009–16 20
2.2 Foreland specialization of top 10 Mediterranean ports, 2015 24
2.3 Traffic concentration among Mediterranean nodes and links, 2009–15 26
2.4 Share of intra-Mediterranean traffic, direct/adjacent and all calls, 2009–16 26
2.5 Intra-Mediterranean traffic distribution by subregional maritime range, all calls, 2009–16 27
2.6 Average traffic size and standard deviation of traffic growth rates in the Mediterranean, 2009–15 29
2.7 Vulnerability and traffic volume of Mediterranean ports, 2015 32
2.8 Subnetworks in the Mediterranean, 2015 33
2.9 Vessel turnaround times in the Mediterranean for all vessels and post-Panamax-plus vessels, 2009–16 (number of days) 35
2.10 Average vessel turnaround time versus number of vessel calls in the Mediterranean, 2009–16 35
2.11 Principal components analysis of Mediterranean ports, 2015 37
2.12 Global versus local connectivity of Mediterranean ports, 2015 38

2A.1 Methodology of network construction from Lloyd's List Intelligence data 39
3.1 Travel time on the main port access road, Algeciras (Spain) and Piraeus, 2016 52
3A.1 The all-road versus feedering costs of a region 63
4.1 Likelihood of choosing a port and port throughput 72
5.1 Three port development paths and strategies 86
5.2 Typology of port connectivity 88

Maps

1.1 Trade routes in the Roman Empire 2
1.2 Global trade flows, 2009–16 2
1.3 Shipping patterns in the Mediterranean, 2009–16 3
1.4 Shipping routes and diversion distances in the Mediterranean, 2015 3
2.1 Share of extra-Mediterranean traffic in total traffic at Mediterranean ports, 2015 21
2.2 Share of Mediterranean traffic at non-Mediterranean ports, 2009–15 22
2.3 Mediterranean and other transshipment regions 23
2.4 Optimal trajectory (trunk line) with the least diversion distance 25
2.5 Traffic volume and share of alliance-related traffic, 2015 25
2.6 Six port clusters grouped according to traffic trajectory 30
3.1 Barcelona's hinterland network, 2010 53
3.2 Inland nodes served by Marseilles port, 2016 56
3.3 Proposed new facilities to expand the hinterland of East Port Said 58
3.4 Tanger Med is two ports in one 59
B3A.1.1 Two hinterlands for Tanger Med, model result, based on 2016 data 65
4.1 Regions of Spain 70

Tables

1.1 Examples of trade connectivity models 9
1.2 Container and roll-on, roll-off volume for short-sea, selected European countries, 2015 11
1.3 Liner shipping connectivity index values in the Mediterranean 14
1A.1 Full menu of port performance indicators, with country- and port-level indicators 15
2.1 Mediterranean network patterns, 2009–16 28
2C.1 Total vessel traffic, 2009–16 41
2C.2 Betweenness centrality, 2009–16 42
2C.3 Degree centrality, 2009–16 43
2C.4 Clustering coefficient, 2009–16 44
3.1 Indicators of hinterland connectivity 48
3.2 Hinterland volume of selected Mediterranean ports, 2015 48
3.3 Modal split of selected Mediterranean ports, 2015 49
3.4 Intermodal connectivity of selected Mediterranean ports, 2016 50
3.5 Container traffic statistics for Barcelona 54
3.6 Inland volume and modal split of Marseilles 55
B3A.1.1 Road distance matrix between all regions and the main ports of Morocco 64
B3A.1.2 Maritime distance and maritime connectivity with four world regions 65
4.1 Traffic of main container ports in Spain, 2016 70
4.2 Subset of coefficients that influence the likelihood of choosing a port 71
4.3 Traffic of Egyptian ports, 2015 73
4.4 Container truck tariffs from ports to the Cairo metropolitan area, 2013 74
4.5 Industrial zones in Tanger Med 77
4A.1 Intermodal connectivity of the port of Algeciras (Spain), 2016 81
4A.2 Distances in nautical miles from Spanish ports to four main world regions 81
4A.3 Estimation of the port choice model for Spain 82
B.1 Performance indicators, Alexandria, 2016 96
B.2 Performance indicators, Algeciras, 2016 96

B.3	Performance indicators, Algiers, 2016	97
B.4	Performance indicators, Ambarli, 2016	97
B.5	Performance indicators, Benghazi, 2016	98
B.6	Performance indicators, Casablanca, 2016	98
B.7	Performance indicators, Genoa, 2016	99
B.8	Performance indicators, Gioia Tauro, 2016	99
B.9	Performance indicators, Marsaxlokk, 2016	100
B.10	Performance indicators, Marseilles, 2016	100
B.11	Performance indicators, Mersin, 2016	101
B.12	Performance indicators, Piraeus, 2016	101
B.13	Performance indicators, Port Said, 2016	102
B.14	Performance indicators, Radès, 2016	102
B.15	Performance indicators, Sines, 2016	103
B.16	Performance indicators, Tanger Med, 2016	103
B.17	Performance indicators, Valencia, 2016	104

Foreword

Maritime Networks, Port Efficiency, and Hinterland Connectivity in the Mediterranean is an opportunity for me to reaffirm how greater regional integration is essential to achieving peace and stability in the Middle East and North Africa Region (MENA). I recognize that this is easier said than done in such a challenging regional and global environment, but make no mistake: it is now that cooperation in the Mediterranean is needed the most. Greater cooperation can help address the roots of instability in the region, as well as deal with the immediate consequences of migration and refugees, and provide knowledge and access to global markets in the long-term. More integration will promote trade and new economic and social policies that will create jobs and foster sustainable growth.

This book provides a rigorous assessment of one of the complex pieces of this urgent agenda. It studies the network of maritime transport across the Mediterranean, a subject of economic and social interests dating back centuries.

Due to its position in global trade, the Mediterranean indeed remains a laboratory of the global hub-and-spoke network pattern. It hosts the port of Tanger Med and the now expanded Suez Canal on the southern rim, two examples of the massive investments in transport and logistics infrastructure that we have seen in the 21st century. Yet fundamental questions still remain to be answered: What are the values and the benefits of global connectivity? What are the economic benefits of massive investments in infrastructure often financed by taxpayers? I often hear these two questions when I meet with government officials across the region. Hubs are critical for transshipment, but risk becoming an economic enclave. What do we need to do to make sure excellent global connectivity translates into economic opportunities for people and firms in the natural hinterland?

This book is the first to tackle these obvious but essential questions. It is valuable to policy makers and private partners who look for solutions to unleash hinterland development. It provides cross-cutting knowledge in transportation and trade. It combines empirical work and experience with a series of case studies, addressing the complex relationship between maritime networks, port efficiency, and hinterland connectivity.

Because of the urgency of what is at stake for the Mediterranean and global communities, *Maritime Networks, Port Efficiency, and Hinterland Connectivity in the Mediterranean* provides a timely piece of rigorous analytical work. I look forward to witnessing its ripple effects across the Mediterranean in the policy discussions that we must have.

Hafez Ghanem
Vice President
Middle East and North Africa
The World Bank

Preface

> Carved out millions of years before mankind reached its coasts, the Mediterranean Sea became a "sea between the lands" linking opposite shores once human beings traversed its surface in search of habitation, food or other vital resources.
>
> —David Abulafia

For millennia the Mediterranean[1] has been a place of trade, where ports and sea routes sustain the prosperity of city-states and their economic hinterlands. Politics, shifts in trade routes, and competition for influence by cities, states, and empires at the rim have influenced the growth and decline of the economies around the sea.

Several of the greatest students of history, following Fernand Braudel,[2] have produced keen insights on growth patterns at the nexus between history and economics. The extraordinarily rich example of the Mediterranean guided and inspired this endeavor in the last century. Braudel and his followers observed that the Mediterranean is the cradle of modern trade and the first example of globalization within its area of influence, even before the industrial revolution. The Mediterranean was the foremost example of an earlier world economy. It is more than its sea routes: it is an extended network of maritime and hinterland routes and trading centers.

Many of today's ports are in the same spots as—or very close to—the trade hubs of antiquity or the Middle Ages. Take Tunisia: the country's main port, Radès, is close to the current capital, Tunis, and even closer to Carthage, the formidable trading and military city-state of the mid-first millennium B.C.E. Carthage was linked to the rest of Mediterranean and outposts in Western Europe and West Africa. Although the Romans destroyed the city at the end of the Third Punic War, the old port that was the hub of Mediterranean (and wider) trade some 25 centuries ago is still visible. Where the quiet public park there now sits may have been the closest thing at the time to today's trade powerhouses of Long Beach, Rotterdam, or Shanghai. The port was the hub of a huge wheel that hosted and served merchant and fighting ships.

How times change. Radès may now have even fewer connections than Carthage used to have. Instead of being the trade center of one of the world's leading economies, it is a port served mainly by the larger ports or shipping hubs in Italy, Spain, and the Eastern Mediterranean and is connected by ferries with a few destinations in France and Italy. Thus Tunisia has direct links only to its closest European trade partners. How to improve the performance of this system and catalyze the international integration of local firms is a central concern of Tunisian policy makers, who have been considering building a deep-sea port to attract large ships operating over long distances.

Further west, Morocco has invested heavily in a major container transshipment hub at Tanger Med on the Strait of Gibraltar. It is extending the hub and building a similar hub on the Nador Peninsula, across the strait from Almeria in Spain. These investments connect Morocco globally, but do they create opportunities in the Moroccan economy beyond direct jobs in the port community? Policy makers in Morocco and in virtually every other country investing in maritime capacities expect the hinterland to enjoy the benefits of connectivity improvements, which go far beyond port investment to include a range of interventions and policy options such as local investment, spatial policies, and industrial policies. Tanger Med is generally viewed as a success: it helped attract foreign investment and generate new manufacturing activities, including the first export-oriented automotive cluster in Africa.

Today trade connectivity in the Mediterranean combines lessons from the past identified by economic historians with 21st century approaches. The Mediterranean is no longer a world economy in itself but a link in the global chain of trade, a place of transit for global container shipping organized around China, Singapore, the Panama Canal, the Strait of Gibraltar, and the Suez Canal. Its sea routes no longer operate on a point-to-point system within the rim but as a hub-and-spoke system where local shipping links transshipment hubs to regional ports. Such hubs are at the eastern and western ends of the Mediterranean (the Arab Republic of Egypt, Morocco, and Spain), and at the pivot between the east and west (around Sicily). Maritime capacity is being built in Southern Mediterranean countries, massively so in Morocco and Egypt, but because of limited financial resources, these countries are highly concerned with their investment returns and the resulting benefits. Major initiatives from farther afield are re-enforcing the need to get these policy options right, such as China's One Belt, One Road, whose investments in main trade routes include the Mediterranean.

These policy considerations inspired this report. It does not aim to be an encyclopedia of maritime patterns or of economic development in Mediterranean countries but a practical exploration of the links among maritime networks and trade, ports, and hinterland development. It defines trade connectivity and its components at different levels: global, port, and hinterland. It explores the policy dimensions of trade connectivity with a focus on maximizing impact. The Mediterranean is a useful laboratory to understand patterns and policies—an understanding that can be profitably used elsewhere—as it combines rich maritime and trade patterns, has economies that differ in development and connectivity, and displays varying policies and outcomes for hinterland development.

The report is intended for a wide readership of policy makers in maritime affairs, trade, or industry; professionals from the world of finance or development institutions; and academics. It combines empirical analysis of microeconomic shipping and port data with three case studies of choice of port (focusing on Spain, Egypt, and Morocco) and five case studies on hinterland development (Barcelona; Malta; Marseilles; Port Said East, Egypt; and Tanger Med, Morocco).

NOTES

1. From the Latin words *medius* (middle) and *terra* (earth or land). In this report, the Mediterranean goes beyond all coastal countries bordering the Mediterranean Sea to include parts of the Atlantic Iberian Peninsula from southwestern Spain up to north Portugal and Atlantic Morocco down to the Casablanca port cluster. It also includes western Black Sea ports in Bulgaria, Romania, Turkey, and Ukraine (to the port of Yuzhny). This extended definition is useful to grasp essential features of recent port dynamics, such as the development of a new container port at Sines (Portugal) in the mid-2000s, the rivalry between Casablanca and Tangier, and the growth of transshipment activities at eastern Mediterranean ports tied to the expansion of Black Sea ports.
2. Fernand Braudel (1902–85) was a French historian who deeply influenced historical sciences in the second half of the 20th century. His landmark books *Mediterranean* and *Civilization and Capitalism* pioneered the study of socioeconomic factors as history drivers.

REFERENCES

Abulafia, D. 2013. *The Great Sea*. Oxford, UK: Oxford University Press.

Braudel, F. 2009. *La Méditerranée : l'espace et l'histoire*. Paris: Flammarion.

Acknowledgments

This publication was led by Jean-François Arvis and Vincent Vesin. The other authors include Robin Carruthers, César Ducruet, and Peter de Langen. This work was a collaboration between the Macroeconomics, Trade and Investment Global Practice, and the Transport and Digital Development Global Practices at the World Bank. The authors would like to thank the following Practice Managers for their guidance: Olivier Le Ber, José-Guillerme Reis, and Nicolas Peltier. The authors would also like to thank for their support the management of the Middle East and North Africa Region at the World Bank led by Vice President Hafez Ghanem.

This book would not be possible without the guidance and input of many colleagues at the World Bank, in the maritime professions, or in academia. They include Cordula Rastogi, Christina Wiederer, Vickram Cuttaree, Chaymae Belaoui, Olivier Hartmann, Matias Herrera, Gerald Ollivier, Jean-Paul Rodrigue, Jamal Benjelloun, Mehdi Tazi, Said Elhadi, Antoine Fremont, Lori Tavasszy, Jan Hofmann, Marie Metge, Zineb Benkirane, Justin Berli and Mattia Bunel.

About the Authors/Editors

Jean-François Arvis, a Senior Economist with the International Trade Department at the World Bank, has been leading the development of advisory work, indicators, and knowledge products in the area of logistics, connectivity, and networks. Prior to joining the Bank, he worked in senior positions with the French Ministry of Economy and Industry (regulation, trade, finance, and development aid). He is a graduate of the École Normale Supérieure in Paris and École Nationale Supérieure des Mines, and holds a doctorate degree in physics.

Robin Carruthers has a first degree in economics and political institutions, a master's degree in statistics, and is a member of the Chartered Institute of Transport and Logistics. Following two decades as Transport Consultant in Australia, Europe, and South America, he joined the World Bank as a Transport Economist. At the Bank, he managed transport and logistics-related projects and studies in each of its six regions, and he supervised its worldwide transport economics activities. He retired from the Bank in 2003. Since then he has been an independent consultant to the United Nations, the World Bank, all the regional development banks, other development agencies, and private companies active in developing countries. He is currently supporting the World Bank in its advice on transport and logistics strategies for Saudi Arabia and Jordan and on road pricing in the United Arab Emirates.

César Ducruet, geographer, is Research Director at the French National Centre for Scientific Research, Paris. His work focuses on transport geography and network science with applications to Europe and Asia. Working as an expert for various organizations—the Organisation for Economic Co-operation and Development, World Bank, Korea Maritime Institute, and Japan External Trade Organization (JETRO)—he is currently the Principal Investigator of the World Seastems research project funded by the European Research Council (2013–19). He recently edited two books, Maritime Networks (2015) and Advances in Shipping Data Analysis and Modeling (2017) in the Routledge *Studies in Transport Analysis* series, in addition to authoring many articles about related matters in peer-reviewed journals.

Peter de Langen is the owner and principal consultant of Ports & Logistics Advisory, and he is Visiting Professor at Copenhagen Business School. de Langen held a part-time position as Professor, Cargo Transport & Logistics, at Eindhoven University of Technology (2009-16), and worked at Port of Rotterdam Authority (2007-13). de Langen is Co-Director of the knowledge dissemination platform, "http://www.porteconomics.eu" www.porteconomics.eu. Since 2016, de Langen has worked in various projects as consultant for the World Bank.

Vincent Vesin is a Senior Transport Specialist at the World Bank in Washington, DC. He joined the World Bank in 2008 and has been leading projects and studies in North Africa, West Africa, and the Middle East in the road, airport, and port sectors. Vesin's current primary interests center around regional integration, rural mobility, and climate resilience. He is a graduate of École Polytechnique in Paris and holds master's degrees in engineering from École Nationale des Ponts et Chaussées (now called École des Ponts ParisTech) in Paris, and the University of Michigan. Prior to joining the World Bank, he worked in aviation in the private sector.

Executive Summary

The Mediterranean has been one of the most active trading areas for millennia. Trade—and by extension connectivity—between Mediterranean riparian countries is one of the oldest and most studied topics in economic history. The Mediterranean has complex trade patterns and routes—but with key differences from the past. It is no longer an isolated world economy: it is both a trading area and a transit area linking Europe and North Africa with the rest of the world through the hub-and-spoke structure of maritime networks (see chapter 1).

Understanding how trade connectivity works in the Mediterranean, and elsewhere, is important to policy makers, especially those in developing countries in the Mediterranean, concerned with the economic benefits of large investment in infrastructure. Better connectivity is expected to increase trade with distant markets and stimulate activities in the hinterland. The interconnectedness of shipping and trade networks means that benefits in one place depend on global and regional patterns. However, local intervention can enhance those benefits. Lessons from the Mediterranean may prove relevant to other regions, so this report was undertaken with both a regional focus and globally scalable lessons in mind.

DIMENSIONS, DRIVERS, AND INDICATORS OF TRADE CONNECTIVITY

Trade connectivity has three interdependent dimensions—maritime networks (also referred to as shipping networks), which refer to the structure and performance of shipping before the port; port efficiency, which refers to the performance of the port (or group of ports sharing the same hinterland); and hinterland connectivity, which involves multiple players and institutions contributing to economic development and exploiting maritime supply chains (figure ES.1). Policies that work well for one dimension can have a positive impact on the others; policies that take all three dimensions into account have greater impact than policies that focus on a single dimension.

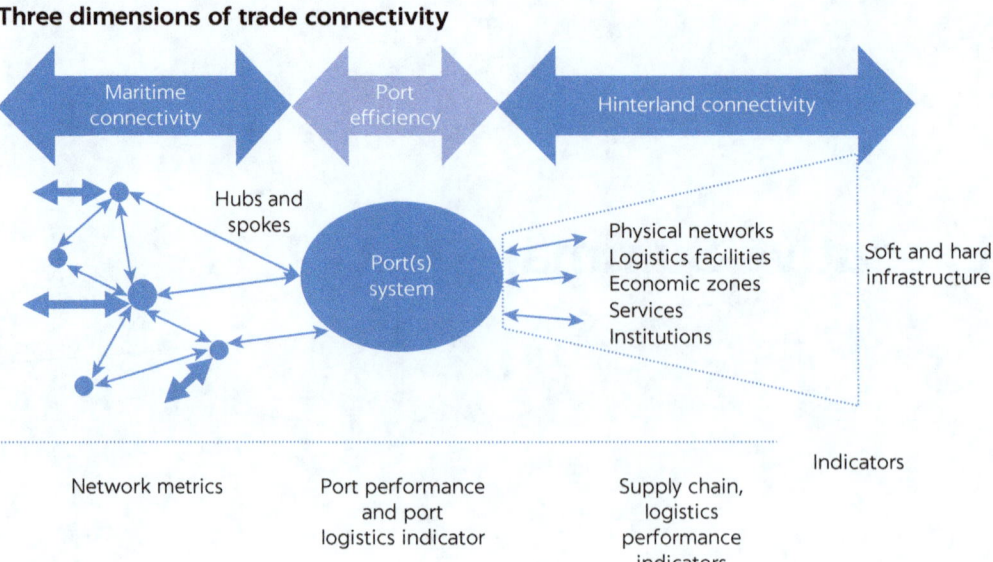

FIGURE ES.1 Three dimensions of trade connectivity

Maritime networks in the Mediterranean have their own hierarchy, with a pronounced distinction between hub and gateway ports (see chapter 2). Hub ports all have a low diversion distance from the Mediterranean's maritime trunk line, the optimal shipping route between the Strait of Gibraltar and the Suez Canal. The number of transshipment hubs suggests intense competition for transshipment cargo: while ports in Africa are closest to the main shipping routes, most transshipment ports are in Europe—with the notable exception of Tanger Med (Morocco) and Port Said East (the Arab Republic of Egypt)—pointing to major transshipment opportunities along the North Africa shore. Gateway ports in the Mediterranean serve the same role as they do elsewhere: they are the maritime trade gateways to their hinterlands, accounting for most of their hinterland's containerized trade.

Maritime networks in the Mediterranean, particularly those in the Western Mediterranean, also use networks of roll-on, roll-off vessels to transport much the same mix of products that is moved in containers. Roll-on, roll-off is especially important for trade between Africa and Europe. Intermodal connectivity should be important for gateway ports but is very limited, except for Marseilles.

Container-terminal productivity differs widely across ports. It improves with throughput volume because it rises with ship size (more cranes can be used at the same time on larger ships) and with call size (the number of containers handled per vessel), enabling more-efficient operations. The productivity of the landlord port model (where container terminals are leased or concessioned to private operators) is higher than that of the public sector port model (where terminals are operated directly by the port authority).

The three dimensions of trade connectivity have complementary drivers of growth and efficiency. The main drivers for each dimension tend to differ, but some address more than one dimension.

The main drivers of maritime networks are industry strategies by shipping lines. Major players such as CMA CGM, Maersk, and Mediterranean Shipping Company (along with Asian, especially Chinese, companies), have been consolidating their operations and are pushing for a hub-and-spoke port system. Such a system also involves regionally focused shipping lines that feed secondary ports in the Mediterranean.

The main drivers of policy interventions for port efficiency have been port and terminal operators implementing new port management methods, developing public–private partnerships, and improving port logistics and trade facilitation.

The main drivers of hinterland connectivity are national and regional governments, through their regional and economic strategies. Government actions include implementation of hard and soft infrastructure interventions, such as connecting infrastructure to existing economic growth poles and setting up industrial and logistics export-oriented facilities (for example, special economic zones). Port authorities are also drivers: they look to extend their port's outreach by making arrangements with and investing in the facilities of operators of inland terminals, logistics zones, and rail networks and by actively promoting their services in areas beyond their traditional hinterland (see chapter 3).

THE MEDITERRANEAN'S MARITIME NETWORKS

The Mediterranean has polycentric but increasingly centralized maritime networks. This centralization reflects a strong east–west divide, with port connectivity differing greatly in scale and scope across the largest ports. Traffic from major shipping alliances appears to be an important driver of maritime connectivity and port efficiency. Maritime networks have a global and local scale (see chapter 2).

Global networks

For direct/adjacent vessel movements between ports, a port's proximity to the trunk line is a strong determinant of extra-Mediterranean traffic (that is, to ports outside the Mediterranean) for transshipment hubs and a few gateways. When all routes and services are included, the diversion distance to the trunk line is compensated for by the gateway effect, which is the ability to connect a port's hinterland, as with Western Mediterranean ports.

The connectivity of the Mediterranean's transshipment ports is geographically more diversified than that of its gateway ports in the distribution of traffic to and from extra-Mediterranean regions. Some ports specialize—for example, Piraeus (Greece) focuses on East Asia, and Sines (Portugal) focuses on Latin America. Shipping alliance traffic is concentrated along the trunk line, while the largest shipping companies and ports are more diversified.

Local networks

As Mediterranean shipping centralizes services, it is becoming more uniform and offering fewer alternatives for main port calls. The share of intra-Mediterranean traffic (that is, to ports within the Mediterranean) in total Mediterranean traffic is increasing, with the majority of intra-Mediterranean traffic going between European ports (mainly east–west). Subnetworks also show a strong east–west divide, with Piraeus–Ambarli (Turkey) and Marsaxlokk (Malta)–Valencia (Spain) the respective central nodes.

Yet the Mediterranean's regional shipping integration is looser than that in more mature areas, such as Northern Europe and North America's East Coast. Expansionwise, some port clusters are showing fast growth around straits, while time efficiency (measured by vessels' average turnaround time) for Mediterranean ports is generally improving, though it is declining for some.

GEOGRAPHIC PATTERNS IN THE MEDITERRANEAN

Large ports are more central, often perform better on average ship turnaround time, and are closer to the trunk line than are smaller ports. Extra-Mediterranean traffic and alliance traffic are also key (but not determining) features of most large ports. Algeciras (Spain), Marsaxlokk (Malta), Tanger Med (Morocco), Sines (Portugal), Damietta (Egypt), and Cagliari (Italy) are among the largest and most central ports and are better located but less attractive to alliances. Ambarli (Turkey), Koper (Slovenia), and Trieste (Italy) are more peripheral but have a higher share of alliance traffic, though their role is more local, and they act as gateways.

Ports situated at the edge of the Mediterranean, such as those along the Strait of Gibraltar and the Black Sea, perform better globally (at the world scale) than locally (at the Mediterranean scale), on the basis of betweenness centrality, because their local centrality within the Mediterranean is cut off. Very few ports perform better locally than globally.

PORT EFFICIENCY

Ports make the link between global or regional shipping networks and economic activities in the hinterland. Thus trade connectivity is influenced by how ports handle the supply chain that goes through them. Efficiency in connecting the hinterland to the global market is not easily captured by simple performance indicators such as container throughput or crane productivity. Nor are globally comparable indicators available, except for service time for container ships (see chapter 1).

A case study of Spain shows how port efficiency (specifically port market share) is related to maritime networks and hinterland connectivity from the perspective of supply chain operators. After seven indicators related to port importance and competitive advantage, connectivity between the hinterland and the port, and connectivity between the port and the destination were analyzed, road distance and throughput volume were found to be the main factors in determining a port's market share. For Spain the likelihood of choosing a port is halved for every 150 kilometers that it is away from the hinterland (see chapter 4).

HINTERLAND CONNECTIVITY

Getting a container to or from a port can be as costly as shipping the container to or from its overseas destination or origin. Although maritime container tariffs have fallen dramatically with the introduction of larger container vessels, hinterland access costs have not. As the opportunities for increased market share and growth through improved maritime connectivity are exhausted, ports are focusing on competitiveness, market share, and economic growth through improved hinterland connectivity. But knowing what the hinterland is and how well it is served has generally been subjective. Objective data on hinterland size and access to ports and on the modal split and intermodal connectivity of that access are becoming more important for ports that are seeking to increase demand through lower transport costs and shorter and more-reliable access time. A change in port access can allow countries both to reap the social and environmental benefits of rail and inland waterway barge transport and to reduce pressure on congested access roads. The current share of rail to most Mediterranean ports is zero or close to it, and the number of rail services that expand the hinterland to other countries is even lower (see chapter 3).

A port authority or port development company can expand its hinterland by increasing the attractiveness of intermodal transport. Initiatives include developing partnerships with inland ports, providing new services, and securing intermodal connections between the various terminals in a port. Tanger Med, Morocco (and Port Said East, Egypt, less so), show that shifts in hinterland cargo between ports occur only gradually and require major investment in landside infrastructure. Increased import–export traffic can also help attract export-oriented industrial activities to the port region, spectacularly as with Tanger Med.

The first step to implementing these measures is to address the paucity of data. Few ports publicly report the inland origins and destinations of their containers, the share of containers that are transported by each mode, or data on intermodal connectivity. But recent advances in automated data collection and processing have a huge potential for better measurement of container movement through the hinterland.

IMPROVING CONNECTIVITY

Maritime networks and hinterland connectivity, together with port efficiency, contribute to a port's overall connectivity and competitiveness—not only from the perspective of port operators, but also from the perspective of actual and potential shippers, those responsible for managing economic and trade growth, and operators and managers of transport and logistic networks and services (see chapter 5).

The major challenge in turning better connectivity into economic benefits is to integrate the development of shipping routes and ports with logistics, free-trade, and industrial zones—and more generally with hinterland connectivity. Such development requires good governance and a holistic approach to the three dimensions of connectivity. A development model in which multiple entities make decisions on the basis of their own sphere of influence is unlikely to be effective.

Given the economic benefits of better connectivity for port users and for society at large, policy makers, port managers, and shipping companies are all active in policies and strategies to improve connectivity. While each group can act independently, coordinated actions are more productive.

Patterns of port developments and connectivity

There are three interrelated port development strategies, each of which prioritizes one of three markets that a port can serve—transshipment,[1] the hinterland, and a local captive cargo base—while taking into account the other two.

Although the strategies rely on different mechanisms, the outcomes are similar. For example, more maritime connectivity from transshipment is a platform to expand the hinterland but requires infrastructure and services (figure ES.2). An expanded hinterland or captive cargo base turns a port into a must-call destination. A port with a favorable location in maritime networks and decent capacity and terminal productivity can attract additional transshipment. Better overseas and hinterland connectivity increases the attractiveness of a port for logistics and manufacturing activities, which also require the location to have solid fiscal performance, a strong labor market, and high scores for ease of doing business. A strong captive cargo base provides a basis for expanding the hinterland. Flows directly to the hinterland can be combined with flows generated by local logistics and manufacturing activities. This creates scale economies, especially if rail or barge transport is used. In addition, the economic benefits of infrastructure that connects the port to the hinterland are larger if that infrastructure is used both for transit cargo and for cargo related to the local logistics and manufacturing activities.

Transshipment flows can be attracted relatively quickly because shipping companies can shift traffic from one port to another without major infrastructure investments (beyond a container terminal with enough storage space). Transshipment is rather footloose, especially given the intense competition among numerous hub ports in the Mediterranean. So ports can attract traffic in a short time span but can also lose it in a short time span. A partnership in which a shipping company takes a substantial share of investment in port infrastructure can reduce this volatility.

In contrast, expanding the hinterland generally requires investment in road and rail infrastructure (and in inland waterways for some ports) and thus takes longer to increase connectivity than attracting transshipment traffic does. These investments are generally time-consuming to plan and implement. In addition, shifts of hinterland port traffic do not happen spontaneously or instantaneously: existing supply chains often persist, because switching entails high costs.

Similarly, expanding the captive cargo base is a lengthy process because it requires developing land for logistics and manufacturing, attracting customers

FIGURE ES.2

Three port development paths and strategies

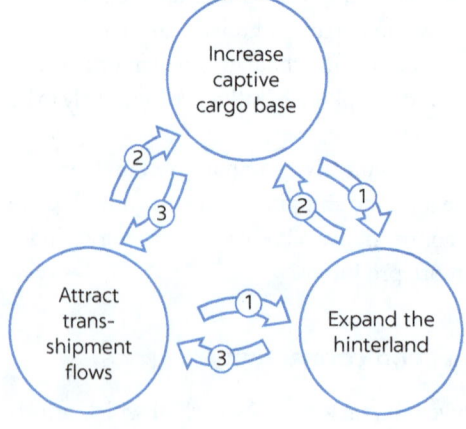

1. **Hinterland expands,** with more maritime connectivity, from transshipment activity and/or when inland destination benefits from the economies of scale of a strong captive cargo base.
2. **Captive cargo increases** as better maritime and hinterland connectivity expand the market potential of logistics and production activity in the port vicinity.
3. **Transshipment develops** as hinterland and/or captive cargo activities expand because the port becomes more attractive to call at for shipping lines.

Note: Does not include non-port-related interventions such as investment in maritime safety and security, which also improves connectivity.

to lease or buy that land, and investing in freight capacity. Many ports that start from a local cargo base are in the downtown area of a port city, where land for expansion is scare or expensive. Only after investment in satellite facilities (such as dry ports and logistics zones) and access routes are realized will logistics and manufacturing operations attract additional traffic to the port from inland locations.

A typology of ports by connectivity and development strategy

Port development is both place-dependent (meaning that it depends on starting point—as a transshipment port, a port focused on the hinterland, or a port dependent on a strong cargo base) and path dependent (meaning that it depends on which strategy is prioritized). The preferred strategy for a port depends on its location on two axes of development—hinterland connectivity and maritime connectivity (figure ES.3).

Growing one or both dimensions will increase traffic (indicated by size of the circle in the center). Cell A represents a typical cargo-based port, with a short hinterland connection (indicated by the dotted line in the left of the cell) and only secondary maritime services to other ports, some of which are feeder services to hub ports (indicated by the dotted line in the right of the cell). This type of port represents many ports that have a long history based on serving just the city and metropolitan area in which they are located. Path A→B2→C3 in figure ES.3 shows a development strategy focused exclusively on transshipment,

FIGURE ES.3
Typology of port connectivity

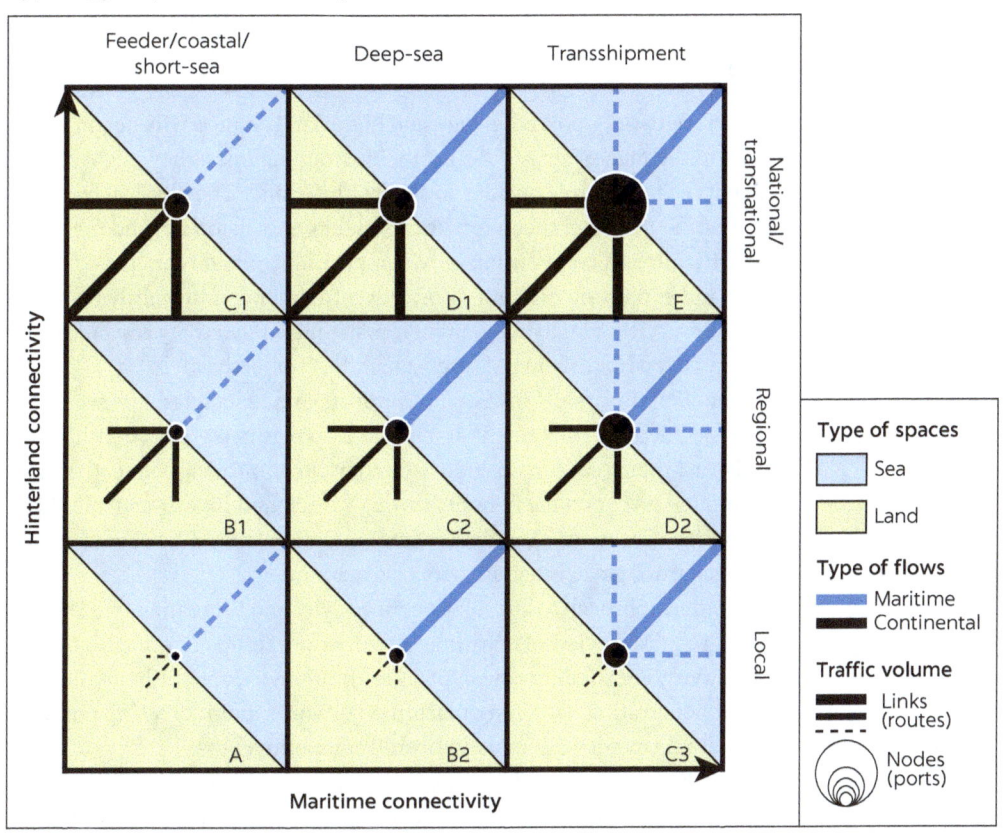

with maritime services evolving from direct and feeder services (A) to one with some transshipment (B2) to one with transshipment and its own feeder services (C3). Path A→B1→C1 shows a development path focused exclusively on hinterland connectivity (including the cargo base), with the hinterland evolving from (A) to an expanded cargo base (B1, with a heavier land connectivity line) to expansion in the hinterland beyond the cargo base (C1).

A port that already has a cargo base (B1 in figure ES.3) and aims to develop transshipment service would add some transshipment services (C2) and ultimately have a stronger cargo base and more balanced demand (D2) than a pure transshipment port.

A pure transshipment port (C3 in figure ES.3) that focused on hinterland development would evolve towards (D2) and then (E), while the most balanced profile (C2) could follow the same path but from a different initial configuration. The (D2) type is more specialized in maritime flows but improves its hinterland connectivity when evolving from (C3) and attracts transshipment activities when evolving from (C2). By contrast a pure cargo base and hinterland port (C1) focused on transshipment would attract more direct calls from shipping lines or deep-sea services (D1) and eventually become a fully-fledged transportation hub with both sea–land and sea–sea transshipment in addition to serving the expanding local cargo base (E). The type (E) can be considered the ultimate stage of development for any port, but many factors come into play that can, after reaching a critical mass, cause connectivity losses on either the hinterland or maritime side (such as congestion, handling costs, lack of space, and port competition and selection). Reverse trajectories are thus also possible.

POLICY RECOMMENDATIONS

General

- Maritime networks, port efficiency, and hinterland connectivity not only contribute to the market shares of a port with shipping lines; they might also be tied to its economic role and the size of its hinterland. The physical fragmentation of the Mediterranean territories makes expansion beyond the cargo base difficult, and competition between port hinterlands can make further hinterland expansion difficult. Most ports that depend primarily on transshipment services aim to build on their maritime connectivity advantage and develop a deep hinterland but rarely meet these objectives.
- The benefits of physical investment in ports and associated investment in land access depend partly on interventions by policy makers not only in ports, but also in other areas such as industry and trade. Improving connectivity and maximizing its economic benefits through trade and investment should be core policy objectives. Any development project should be rooted in and envisaged through an integrated port cluster strategy.
- A consistent approach to improving connectivity and to creating trade opportunities requires review of maritime networks, port efficiency, and hinterland connectivity. For Mediterranean ports with limited scope for increased hinterland penetration, widening maritime networks and increasing port efficiency are the main ways to boost overall competitiveness.
- Policy makers need to consider improvements in maritime networks, port efficiency, and hinterland connectivity to be interdependent. National policies

have little direct leverage on maritime networks, which are driven largely by the strategies of global shipping lines, but can affect port efficiency or hinterland connectivity, which could in turn influence maritime networks. One potential strategy is to attract vertically integrated shipping companies that are also involved in inland logistics and terminal operations.
- Port development strategies are often part of a national trade development strategy. Although the link between maritime networks and hinterland connectivity have been demonstrated, more research is needed to better understand the links and causations among maritime networks, port efficiency, hinterland connectivity, and trade outcomes.
- Successful strategies of port expansion are usually location and path specific and cannot simply be transposed to or replicated at another port. To pursue an optimal port development path, policy makers need to take into account local, regional, and national considerations—and even historical and cultural ones. The strategies indicated here provide a framework that includes maritime networks, port efficiency, and hinterland connectivity, within which more-specific port development paths can be determined.

Maritime networks and port efficiency

- Mediterranean container ports show clear economies of scale, as evidenced by those in Spain. Volume is also closely related to higher maritime connectivity—scale economies partly explain the increasing concentration of shipping line calls in the Mediterranean. To take scale economies into account, policy makers could focus on one or a few core ports and core corridors. Cross-border cooperation between ports and countries should also be envisaged to avoid overcapacity.
- From the perspective of trade connectivity, port efficiency requires port reform (involving the landlord, operators, and shipping lines) and trade facilitation (customs, border agencies, and freight forwarders). A good balance and dialogue are necessary between global and local players, but bringing in global alliances might not yield immediate benefits unless the alliances are well integrated with the local port community.
- Policy makers are generally aware of where applying best practices could do the most to improve the efficiency of gateway ports (port management reforms and trade facilitation). However, outcomes of the application of best practices vary greatly across Mediterranean countries and ports—with North African ports benefitting the least.
- Given the importance of all three dimensions of trade connectivity in increasing port competitiveness, more data on connectivity—including data on port efficiency and hinterland destinations of containers—are needed to ensure efficient and effective application of best practices. And improving the comparability of data across ports requires partnerships among providers of connectivity data and cross-border cooperation.
- Roll-on, roll-off services generally complement container services, because roll-on, roll-off is faster and generally does not entail transshipment. To be comprehensive, development strategies should go beyond container connectivity to include maritime connectivity through roll-on, roll-off services. Balanced development of port maritime networks would take into account regional and local connectivity, as through short-sea and coastal shipping, as well as roll-on, roll-off and global maritime connectivity.

Hinterland connectivity

- Policy initiatives targeting the hinterland are needed to boost the impact of maritime networks, especially improving the value of transshipment hubs for national and regional economies. Otherwise transshipment supports only offshore activities, with few economic links to the hinterland
- Development of hinterland connectivity is most efficiently pursued through a regionalization strategy based on inland port development and value-added logistics
- Captive cargo bases can best be implemented through policies that have both hard and soft components. Such policies include those that focus on developing logistics and trade-oriented manufacturing clusters (such as special economic zones) that are well-linked (if not adjacent) to the port complex. and those that focus on improving hinterland access, as is being done in Tanger Med, Morocco (and is being attempted in Port Said, Egypt)
- Getting hinterland governance right is critical for developing logistics and trade-oriented manufacturing clusters near ports. Tanger Med (Morocco) is close to being a best-practice port where an integrated development approach has worked well (in contrast to Port Said East, Egypt, where a nonintegrated approach has failed to add hinterland trade to an otherwise successful transshipment port). Even in successful cases, integrated development is a long-term endeavor
- A hinterland expansion strategy depends on infrastructure and logistics networks, preferably with rail and road connections, which can bring about the seamless supply chain connections that are essential for success
- Of concern in the Mediterranean is the lack of intermodal connections. Compared with other regions in global trade (East Asia, North America, and Northern Europe), most Mediterranean ports, especially those outside the European Union, have limited or no intermodal connectivity for moving containers to and from their cargo base or hinterland. A small number of ports, some within the European Union, have less need for intermodal connectivity because of their insular location (for example, Marsaxlokk in Malta), but these are exceptions. Barcelona, and to a lesser extent Marseilles, show how attention to intermodal connectivity can increase penetration of a hinterland that faces strong competition from other ports. Improving intermodal connection extends and connects the hinterland and spreads the economic benefits of international trade to inland regions that are otherwise too remote from a port to participate.

NOTE

1. This market can be further segmented into interlining (transfer of containers between mother vessels at the crossroads of the trunk line) and hub-and-spoke (transfer of containers between mother vessels and feeder ships within the region).

Abbreviations

ARD	all-road distance
GDP	gross domestic product
HHI	Herfindahl-Hirschman Index
IHS	Information Handling Services
MFD	maritime feeder distance
PC	port costs
TEU	twenty-foot equivalent unit
VMC	variable maritime costs
VRC	variable road costs

1 Dimensions, Indicators, and Drivers of Trade Connectivity in the Mediterranean

During the Roman Empire, Mediterranean ports brought traded goods from Rome's provinces, according to their resources, to Rome and other places of consumption (map 1.1). A maritime network centered on Ostia (Rome's port) supported this trade. The main nodes in this port system were well linked to their provinces through Roman roads or waterways.

Although today's Rome no longer has a major commercial port nearby, many of the old nodes remain important ports—Alexandria, Barcelona, Carthage (Tunis), Istanbul, Marseilles, and Piraeus (Athens)—that serve wide hinterlands. The precise locations have often shifted to allow modern facilities to be built.

Shipping intensified in the 19th century with the advent of steam and the opening of the Suez Canal, which made the Mediterranean the primary transit route between Europe and Asia. Containerization in the latter part of the 20th century again changed trade patterns, with maritime networks working increasingly through transshipment hubs, major gateways, and feeder ports.[1]

This chapter presents an overview of networks and geographic areas in the Mediterranean region, puts forward a tripartite conceptual framework, considers indicators useful in measuring trade connectivity and the efficiency of the Mediterranean's major ports, and briefly reviews some drivers of trade connectivity.

THE MEDITERRANEAN: THE NEXUS OF WORLD TRADE OR ITS OWN SMALL WORLD?

The Mediterranean today is not a quasi-independent network as it was in antiquity but a major link in the global trade system (map 1.2). The maritime networks in the Mediterranean are structured according to the sea's internal geography and the locations of the main hubs and gateways (map 1.3).

The huge number of ships transiting through the Mediterranean heavily influences the shipping routes in the Mediterranean (see map 1.3). The route toward the Suez Canal is not the biggest for the Mediterranean. Around 70,000 ships a year pass through the Strait of Gibraltar, compared with about 18,000

MAP 1.1
Trade routes in the Roman Empire

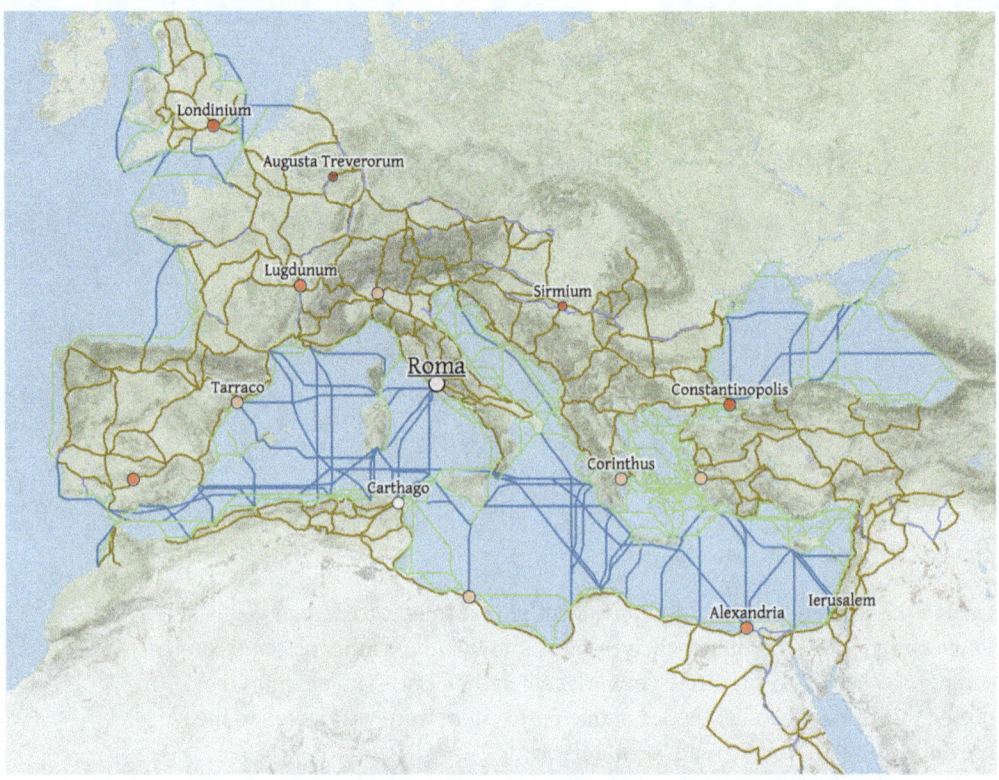

Source: Scheidel and Meeks 2012. This work is available under the Creative Commons Attribution 3.0 IGO license (CC BY 3.0 IGO).
Note: Green lines refer to coastal routes, blue lines refer to open sea routes, brown lines refer to land routes, and purple lines refer to river routes.

MAP 1.2
Global trade flows, 2009–16

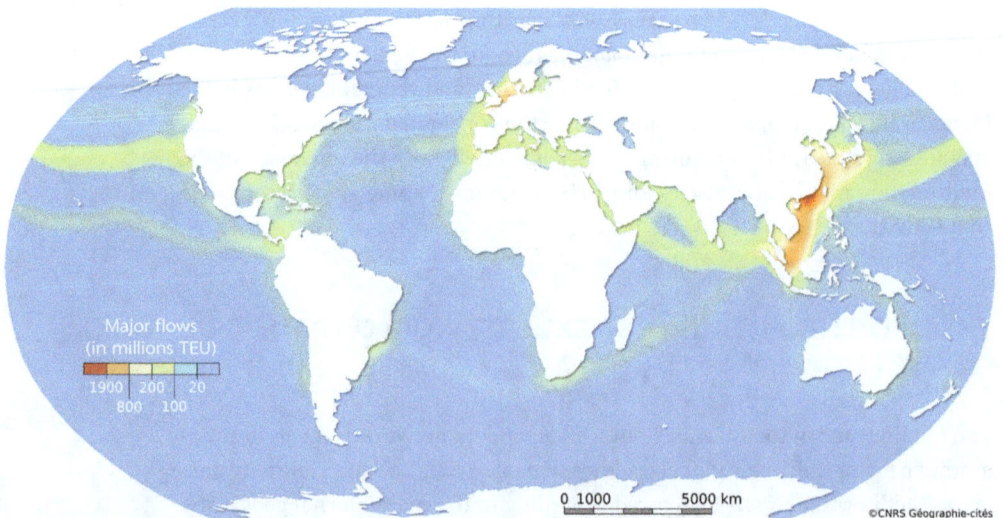

Source: Produced by Justin Berli (Centre national de la recherche scientifique) and Mattia Bunel (Institut national de l'information géographique et forestière) based on data from Lloyd's List Intelligence (see annex 2A).

through the Suez Canal, underlining the large number of ships from the Mediterranean to, for example, the Americas, Northern Europe, and West Africa. Huge numbers of ship movements are purely within the Mediterranean. The imbalance in ship movements is huge between the northern coast of the Mediterranean (Europe) and the southern coast (Africa), with many more along the European coast because of higher population density and greater economic development (see map 1.3).

For container shipping the Mediterranean's transit role leads to maritime networks with hub ports with low diversion distances (the deviation required from the transit route and feeder ports elsewhere in the Mediterranean; map 1.4).

MAP 1.3

Shipping patterns in the Mediterranean, 2009–16

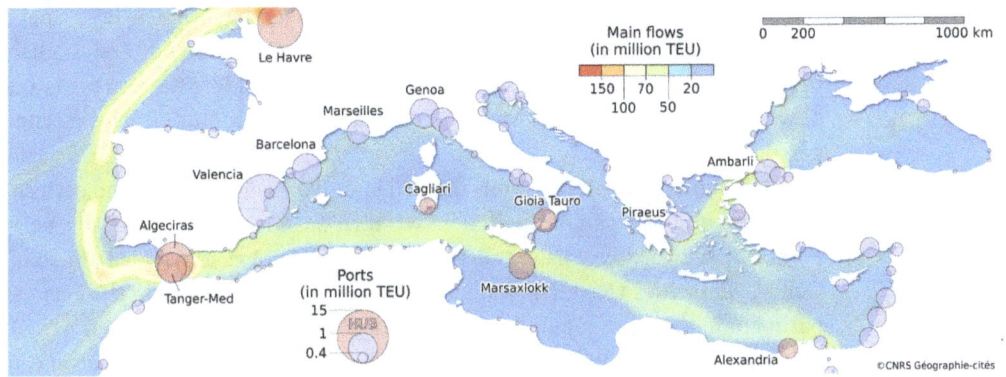

Source: Produced by Justin Berli (Centre national de la recherche scientifique) and Mattia Bunel (Institut national de l'information géographique et forestière) based on data from Lloyd's List Intelligence (see annex 2A).

MAP 1.4

Shipping routes and diversion distances in the Mediterranean, 2015

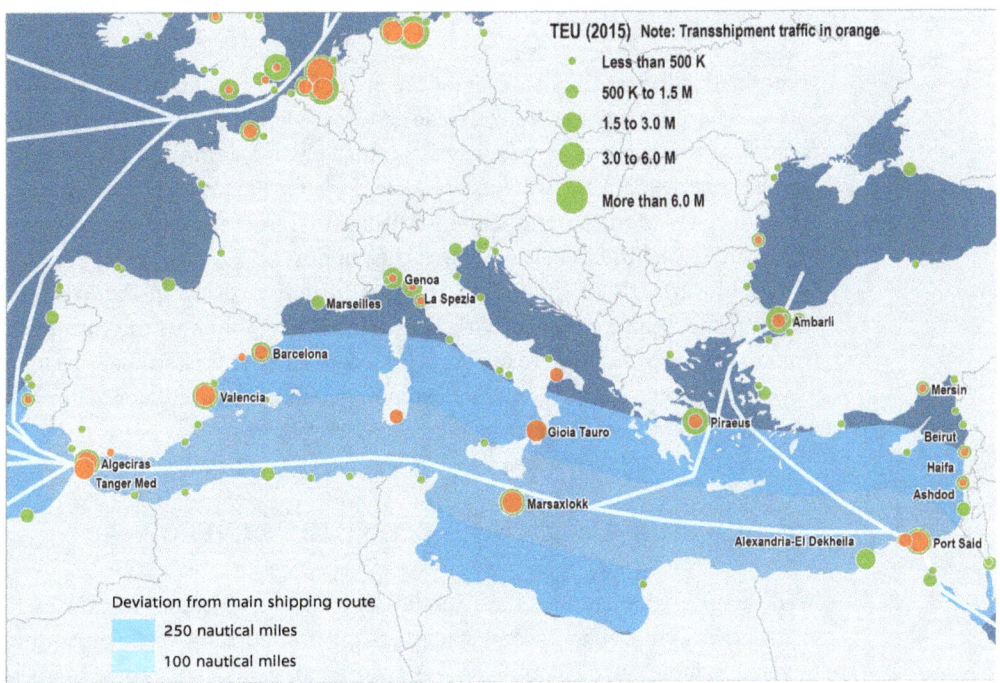

Source: Adapted from Rodrigue, J-P and T. Notteboom (2010).
Note: Orange circles indicate transshipment traffic.

Hub ports are more diversified than gateway ports in foreign ports to which they are connected because of hub ports' transshipment function.

For ports in the Mediterranean, proximity to major shipping routes is an opportunity. Attracting transshipment traffic has a positive effect on a port's maritime connectivity by reducing trade costs and boosting trade. Connectivity also increases a port's attractiveness as a location for logistics value-added services, such as warehousing, repacking, light assembly activities, and customizing. For these reasons policy makers are keen to develop large deep-sea container terminals.

The Mediterranean: port and shipping routes

The geographic area of the Mediterranean includes the sea itself as well as Atlantic ports in Morocco (such as Casablanca), Portugal (Sines), and Spain (Bilbao and Corunna), because they share the same hinterland. The English Channel and the North Sea, the Black Sea, and many Middle Eastern ports are closely connected to the Mediterranean and are included as external partners.

The Mediterranean is naturally divided into two basins, western and eastern, separated by the Strait of Sicily. The western basin serves Algeria, southern France, Italy, Morocco, Spain, and Tunisia; its main gateways include Barcelona, Genoa, Marseilles (Fos), and Valencia (Spain). The main ports in the eastern basin are in the Arab republic of Egypt (Alexandria), Greece (Piraeus), Israel, Lebanon, the Syrian Arab Republic, and Turkey. Seventeen major Mediterranean ports are briefly described in the appendix A. Major transshipment hubs are at the Strait of Gibraltar or relatively close by (Algeciras, Spain; Tangier, Morocco; and Valencia, Spain); at the junction of the two basins (Malta and Sicily); and at the Suez Canal (Port Said, Egypt; see map 1.3).

Hinterland

Hinterland is the traditional term for the area of logistics and economic influence of a port or more generally a trade gateway.[2] On the southern rim the hinterland of the main port gateway is almost always delimited by national boundaries: the main entry points are Alexandria for Egypt, Algiers for Algeria, Casablanca for Morocco, and Radès for Tunisia. Transit across borders is very rare, with only a little from Tunisia to its neighbors.

The hinterlands of the main gateways heavily overlap in the Western Mediterranean and compete with the major entry points to the European Union—Antwerp and Rotterdam. Ports in Greece and the western Balkans tend to serve their own countries but are extending their zones of influence into the landlocked countries of Central and Eastern Europe.

TRADE CONNECTIVITY AND ECONOMIC DEVELOPMENT

Trade connectivity captures the structure, spread, and efficiency of global services networks that enable access to markets and to opportunities. Countries and regions are increasingly identifying it as a key factor in achieving trade competitiveness and sustainable, inclusive economic growth.

The One Belt, One Road initiative, led by China and targeting more than 60 countries, seeks to improve trade connectivity among former Silk Road economies (the Belt) and countries on the main sea routes from China (the Road) to Europe, including the Mediterranean. Still in development, this ambitious program will target physical infrastructure in multiple locations and aims to catalyze finance and investment. The Mediterranean Sea is part of the road. Even before One Belt, One Road, Chinese operators had growing influence over ports and maritime activities in the countries of the Belt, further underlining the global reach of shipping and logistics companies in China. For instance, Chinese operator COSCO has redeveloped the Piraeus gateway.

The Mediterranean lacks a trade connectivity initiative in such a format. The Union for the Mediterranean,[3] founded in 2008, is arguably an initiative of this type, to encourage economic links among countries along the rim. The secretariat of the union is not a funding agency; it is a small structure whose role is to advocate and facilitate, through coordination of countries and financing organizations, important cross-border projects that do not fall the under the responsibility of a single country. The European Commission has extended the transport corridor concept to maritime routes. This initiative is called Motorways of the Sea, and it was proposed as a competitive alternative to land transport for routes linking non-EU countries to European Union (EU) countries in the Mediterranean. It aimed to introduce new intermodal maritime-based logistics chains in Europe in order to improve transport organization (Commission of the European Communities 2001).

Trade connectivity integrates many dimensions and scales: countries in the global economy and regions in countries. Trade, information, freight, logistics, energy, and financial networks all interact. Connectivity is as much about physical connections as it is about services, and it thus depends on policy and investments. At the national level good trade connectivity to hubs of global economic activity is critical to integrating regional and global trade and value chains. Connectivity is enhanced by removing trade barriers and reducing trade costs. At the subnational level regions disconnected economically from dynamic economic centers—but not necessarily geographically distant—have higher trade costs and do not realize market opportunities. Poor links inhibit economic potential and contribute to lower socioeconomic outcomes.

Several researchers (including Jean-Paul Rodrigue and César Ducruet) have studied the relationship among maritime networks, their growth, and their influence on hinterland development. The networks are highly complex systems with many places, modes of transport (bulk; container; roll-on, roll-off), types of services, and regulatory agencies. A natural way to approach this complexity is to look at it from the perspective of the supply chain—and that of a trader or manufacturer in a single Mediterranean country. The supply chain setup with overseas markets (regardless of whether they are also in the Mediterranean) includes logistics in the foreland (that is, in international waters), the logistics at a gateway port, and the logistics system in the hinterland.

Trade connectivity is therefore viewed here along three dimensions: maritime networks, which refers to the structure and performance of shipping networks before the gateway; port efficiency, which refers to the

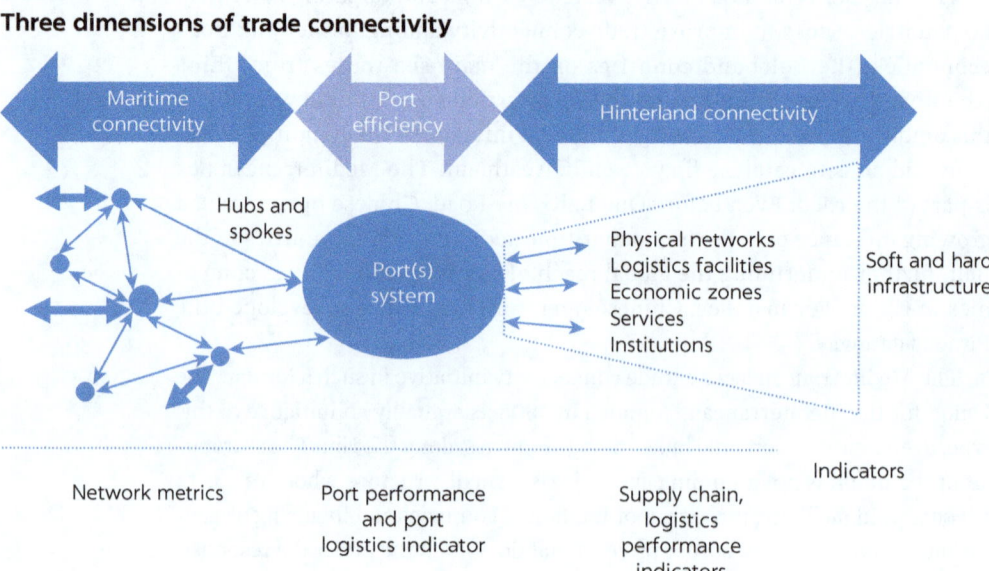

FIGURE 1.1
Three dimensions of trade connectivity

performance of the gateway (a port or group of ports sharing the same hinterland); and hinterland connectivity, which involves multiple players and institutions contributing to economic development and exploiting maritime supply chains (figure 1.1). All three dimensions explain how economies take advantage of their position in global and regional networks (roughly, what connectivity is about).

A distinction can be made between the hub function and the gateway function of a port. The hub function entails a role as transshipment center, where containers arrive by ship and are loaded on another ship. The hub function includes relay traffic, the transfer of containers from one intercontinental service to another (for example in Tanger Med, Morocco, containers on the Asia–Europe trade route are transshipped to the Europe–West Africa trade route) as well as feeder traffic, the delivery of containers to nearby feeder ports, generally with smaller vessels (for instance, containers from Asia are transshipped in Algeciras, Spain, and feeder ships bring the containers to destination ports such as Malaga and Seville). The gateway function is when a port serves as the entrance and exit of merchandise in a region, country, or group of counties.

Some ports combine the hub and gateway functions (the best examples in the Mediterranean being Piraeus and Valencia, Spain), other ports are essentially hubs (Algeciras, Spain; and Tanger Med (Morocco), and still others are essentially gateway ports (Casablanca and Marseille).

There is a fundamental difference between the requirements for hubs and for gateways. Hubs require an efficient container terminal because containers do not leave the fences of the port and customs-related processes are rarely a constraint. By contrast, gateways require a full range of transport and logistics services and efficient hinterland connections to perform efficiently. Therefore, a gateway port can attract hub traffic if it is well located in maritime networks and can attract an anchor shipping company with hub operations in the port. Such a development creates value for the shipping company and terminal operator but has little direct impact on the economic activity in the hinterland. For a hub to also become a gateway, hinterland connections as well as a full range of transport and shipping services need to be developed.

MEASURING TRADE CONNECTIVITY: INDICATORS

Intuitively, connectivity refers to position in trade, shipping, or logistics networks. Despite the popularity of the term "connectivity" in the context of trade and supply chains, there is still no established theoretical framework for it. Nor is there a consensus on how to gauge the economic benefits of connectivity. Understanding the multidimensional nature of trade connectivity is challenging. Take the case of shipping and trade. The cost of trade depends on shipping connectivity: for instance, all else being equal, the trade potential is lower between two countries that lack a direct connection. Among other things transshipment creates delays in the supply chain. Conversely, a growing volume of bilateral trade creates opportunities for better connections (direct routes or larger ships). Frictions that impede flows can be bilateral while including elements of performance at the node level (port or country).

The two most popular indicators of trade connectivity are the United Nations Conference on Trade and Development's Liner Shipping Connectivity Index, which reflects maritime networks' integration on the basis of intuitive industry attributes of network connectivity and applies to the connectivity of the foreland (box 1.1), and the World Bank's Logistics Performance Index, which reflects logistics industry knowledge of how supply chains perform at the gateway and within the country (box 1.2). Although they apply to different dimensions of connectivity, they are quite correlated (Ojala and Hoffman 2010). The causal effects and diffusion of improvements are complex: good logistics is encouraged by good maritime networks, but the reverse may also be true. Both indicators are national indicators and do not describe the efficiency of specific ports.

Building on advances in network science and the growing availability of network data for global services such as shipping and aviation, several researchers have developed trade connectivity indicators (table 1.1).

BOX 1.1

The Liner Shipping Connectivity Index

The *Liner Shipping Connectivity Index* is the most popular indicator of maritime networks. Published annually by the United Nations Conference on Trade and Development since 2004, it is a national (not port-level) index, focusing on container shipping marking integration of national economies in global container shipping networks (figure B1.1.1). Unlike the survey-based *Logistics Performance Index*, the *Liner Shipping Connectivity Index* is constructed from globally available information on shipping routes and shipping activity.[a] The index is heuristic, an intuitive combination of what most experts consider attributes of container shipping connectivity. It consists of normalized averages of indicators on volume, frequency, and diversity of routes. Its main elements are number of ships calling in a country, average and maximum size of ships calling in the country, container throughput, number of services, and number of shipping companies linking to other countries.

(continued)

Box 1.1, continued

FIGURE B1.1.1

Liner Shipping Connectivity Index values for major hubs and gateways, 2004–16
Index, 100 = China in 2004

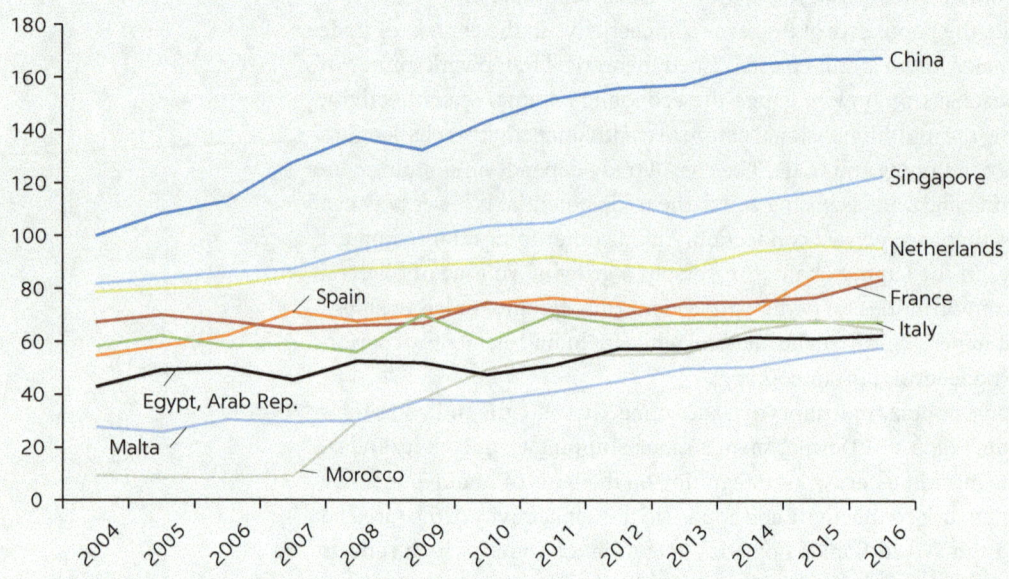

Source: Calculation based on data from the United Nations Conference on Trade and Development's UNCTADstat database (http://unctadstat.unctad.org/wds/TableViewer/tableView.aspx?ReportId=92).
Note: Higher values indicate better connectivity.

The *Liner Shipping Connectivity Index* is very well correlated with other indicators of trade integration. Arvis et al. (2013b) found that maritime networks have the greatest impact on cutting trade costs. Ojala and Hoffman (2010) found that the index was closely associated with logistics performance and backed up the intuition that transshipment may raise trade costs. In 2014, the United Nations Conference on Trade and Development launched the *Liner Shipping Bilateral Connectivity Index*, a second indicator measuring how well a pair of countries are connected.

a. The United Nations Conference on Trade and Development buys shipping schedule data from a private provider, Lloyd's List Intelligence.

BOX 1.2

The Logistics Performance Index

The World Bank's *Logistics Performance Index* is also relevant for measuring trade connectivity. It is a comprehensive index that covered the entire supply chain for 160 countries in 2016. It is based on a biannual survey of nearly 1,000 logistics professionals worldwide and is useful for comparing performance across countries and identifying and prioritizing new interventions within countries. The index has two strands,

(continued)

Box 1.2, *continued*

international (which is most relevant for maritime transport) and domestic, which is based on numerical ratings of 1 (weakest) to 5 (strongest).

The international Logistics Performance Index is a weighted average of six components:

- Efficiency of the clearance process
- Quality of trade- and transport-related infrastructure
- Ease of arranging competitively priced shipments
- Competence and quality of logistics
- Ability to track and trace consignments
- Frequency with which shipments reach the consignee within the scheduled or expected delivery time (figure B1.2.1).

FIGURE B1.2.1

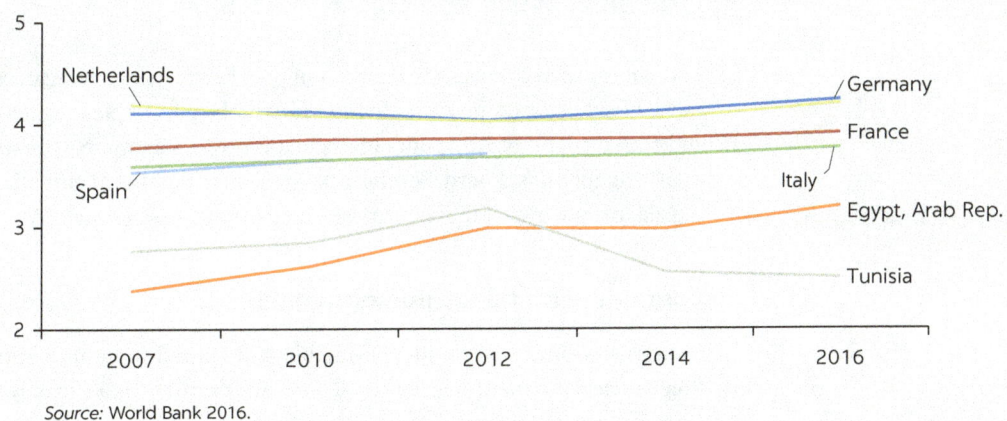

Source: World Bank 2016.

TABLE 1.1 Examples of trade connectivity models

STUDY	METRIC	DESCRIPTION
Hoffman 2005	Liner Shipping Connectivity Index	Average of the normalized values of five components: • Number of container ships on the liner services to and from a country's ports. • Carrying capacity of container ships on the liner services to and from a country's ports (twenty-foot equivalent units). • Maximum vessel size. • Number of services. • Number of companies deploying container ships on services to and from a country's ports.
Tang, Low, and Lam 2011	Port Connectivity or Accessibility Index	Connectivity or accessibility is a function of the number of ports that can be reached directly by the evaluated port, the number of ports that can be reached directly from ports directly connected to the evaluated port, and the number of ports that can be jointly reached directly through both.
Arvis and Shepherd 2011	Air Connectivity Index	Connectivity is defined as the importance of a country as a node within the global air transport system. A country's connectivity score is higher if the cost of moving to other countries in the network is relatively low. This model incorporates network effects—that is, the connectivity of C depends on interaction between A and B.

(continued)

TABLE 1.1, *Continued*

STUDY	METRIC	DESCRIPTION
Maersk 2014	Drewry Liner Shipping Connectivity Index	Average of the four normalized components: • Number of shipping companies. • Twenty-foot equivalent unit carrying capacity. • Calls per shipping company. • Number of services. No major difference from the Liner Shipping Connectivity Index.
Jiang et al. 2015	Port Connectivity Index	The difference in the sum of minimum transportation times along all origins' and destinations' shortest paths in the network.
		The difference in the sums of maximum capacity flows along all origins' and destinations' shortest paths.

USING INDICATORS TO MEASURE PERFORMANCE OF THE MAIN MEDITERRANEAN PORTS

There is no such thing as the right set of port performance indicators. The relevance of indicators depends on the specifics of the port or port region in question[4] and data availability. And poor data availability often hampers attempts to create a performance dashboard. For these two reasons a longlist of potential indicators is used, from which indicators are selected case by case (annex 1A).

Container and transshipment volume

Container volumes are widely available, but transshipment volumes are not. Precise transshipment shares (based on volume) are available in only a few ports. Data on transshipment allow for transshipment ports—where the majority of traffic is transshipment—to be distinguished from gateway ports—where the majority of traffic is to or from inland destinations.

Port or terminal productivity

In the container segment the emerging global standard for port or terminal productivity is the Information Handling Services (IHS) container productivity benchmark. It is a commercial dataset compiled by IHS Markit, a data company from information collected from shipping companies to IHS. The indicator is essentially the time needed to serve ships according to predefine size categories; it provides the productivity of port service from the shipping company perspective.

Roll-on, roll-off volume and services

Roll-on, roll-off shipping is an important transport mode in the Mediterranean (figure 1.1 and table 1.2). While there are no statistics for trade with North Africa, there are statistics for intra-EU trade, which show that in Europe roll-on, roll-off trade is as important for short-sea shipping as containers are. Roll-on, roll-off is not used for deep-sea shipping because roll-on, roll-off is not cost competitive for this segment (since the key feature of roll-on, roll-off is that trucks or trailers, sometimes with drivers, are transported by ship, enabling fast and cheap loading and unloading). However, the disadvantages are that more space is required and that shipping is more expensive. Thus, in addition to the widely used indicators

FIGURE 1.2
Breakdown of modes in total short-sea shipping traffic in European regions, 2015 (%)

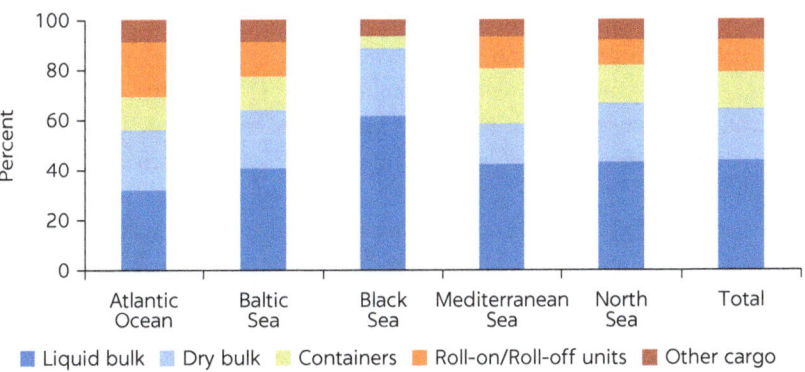

- Liquid bulk
- Dry bulk
- Containers
- Roll-on/Roll-off units
- Other cargo

Source: Eurostat 2017.

TABLE 1.2 Container and roll-on, roll-off volume for short-sea, selected European countries, 2015

COUNTRY	TOTAL (THOUSANDS OF TONS)	LARGE CONTAINERS (NUMBER)	ROLL-ON, ROLL-OFF[a]	
			MOBILE SELF-PROPELLED (NUMBER)	MOBILE NON-SELF-PROPELLED (NUMBER)
European Union (28 countries)	1,844,904	265,183	142,958	109,638
Italy	275,642	53,024	28,805	25,124
Spain	226,854	47,152	9,369	9,150
Turkey	202,122	51,053	6,083	15
France	170,283	10,408	30,252	2,240
Greece	98,055	22,494	11,584	2,516
Portugal	44,909	11,853	247	573
Cyprus	6,929	1,872	40	108
Malta	3,409	486	227	406

Source: Eurostat 2017.
Note: Excludes feeder moves, even if the origin or destination of the container is outside the short-sea shipping region.
a. Self-propelled units refer mainly to trucks; non-self-propelled units refer mainly to trailers not accompanied by a powered vehicle.

for containers, roll-on, roll-off indicators, such as volume and connectivity of the Mediterranean ports can be assessed on the basis of public information on cargo volumes and shipping schedules.

Hinterland connectivity and economic zones

Indicators of hinterland connectivity are discussed in more detail in chapter 3. One important indicator is intermodal connectivity. Intermodal terminals allow for efficient transfer of cargo and containers from one high-volume mode of transportation, such as rail or river barges, to trucks that link to final destinations. The connectivity of intermodal transport thus refers to the number of rail or barge inland terminals that can be reached from a port.

Intermodal connectivity can be calculated when container train and barge[5] schedules are publicly available, which is increasingly the case because publicly providing schedule information is part of the marketing efforts of train and barge service providers to attract individual shippers. This type of data is often available on platforms that have schedule information from multiple service providers (for example, www.intermodallinks.com for Europe). With such data, several methods can be used to express a port's intermodal connectivity. The simplest indicator is the sum of the unique directly served destinations from a port.[6]

Another indicator is the presence of a special economic zone (sometimes referred to as a free zone) in or near the port. Attracting value-added activities to the port is both beneficial for the port region and optimal from a supply chain perspective. Furthermore, virtually all ports develop their own logistics zones, and some ports make them more attractive through special economic status. Though not the appropriate policy instrument in all cases, data on the presence of such zones are included.

Port governance

Even though port governance is not a port performance indicator in the strict sense—that is, it is not an outcome of port activities but a description of how the governance of a port is organized—it is relevant because various studies have shown its effect on outcome indicators such as productivity (Cheon, Dowall, and Song 2010).

Core governance dimensions relate to the business model of the port authority (landlord, with services provided by third parties, or service port, with services provided in house) and the governance structure of the authority. Institutional characteristics influence port performance, and port reform has yielded well-documented benefits in many countries. Two broadly defined reforms have proven beneficial:

- Changing state entities that provide terminal services (public service ports) to landlords, with private specialized companies providing terminal services
- Changing a public port authority from an entity integrated in the public sector to an autonomous state-owned enterprise (De Langen and Heij 2014).[7]
- These governance aspects are included in the port descriptions in annex 1A.[8]

DRIVERS OF TRADE CONNECTIVITY

Maritime networks are the backbone of international trade because most international supply chains depend on ports and container shipping companies for transport (or roll-on, roll-off for short distances). The Mediterranean Sea is the oldest example of such networks. Countries in North Africa and the Eastern Mediterranean depend on the region's maritime connections not only for their trade with Europe and the rest of the world, but also for their intraregional trade because of a lack of cross-hinterland connectivity.

A major goal of policy makers, operators, and financial institutions that invest in maritime networks such as infrastructure and services is to maximize economic returns, not just for one stakeholder (such as the port operator) but for the region or country more widely. Thus the value of connectivity infrastructure such as a transshipment port cannot be assessed purely in financial terms: the impact on trade, competitiveness, and local development must also be taken into account. The three dimensions of connectivity—maritime networks, port efficiency, and hinterland connectivity—have complementary drivers, as analyzed in chapters 2 and 3.

The main drivers of maritime networks have been industry strategy. Major players such as CMA CGM, Maersk, and Mediterranean Shipping Company (along with Asian, especially Chinese, companies) have been consolidating their operations and are pushing for a hub-and-spoke port system (Fremont 2007). Such a system also involves port operators that are not shipping companies and regionally focused shipping companies that feed secondary ports in the Mediterranean. Policy makers have little role in shaping these trends, which are driven by cost reductions, long-term investments (such as larger, post-Panamax ships), and trade demand. Since the 2007/08 global recession, global trade has grown at 2.5 percent per year—slower than global output (WTO 2015). This new normal for trade has major impacts on rationalizing and consolidating the underlying shipping and logistics networks (WTO 2015). However, as Morocco shows, countries can take advantage of these trends by being friendly to investment in hubs.

Conversely, port efficiency is a traditional area of intervention, which combines hard and soft infrastructure. The body of experience in such areas as port management, public–private partnerships, and port logistics and trade facilitation is considerable and well documented. The World Bank has developed a port reform toolkit (World Bank 2003) and a trade and transport corridor management toolkit (Kunaka and Carruthers 2014), so this report does not cover these topics in depth. Instead, it explores the effectiveness of these interventions across regions (on the basis of differences in port performance) as well as new topics such as how gateway performance is tied to maritime networks.

The development of hinterland connectivity in the sense of maximizing the economic benefits of connectivity and port performance is a newer topic. It includes many areas where policy makers or public–private partners may act, with hard and soft infrastructure interventions, such as connecting infrastructure to existing economic growth poles and setting up export-oriented industrial and logistics facilities (for example, special economic zones). Governance and institutions organizing connectivity with the hinterland are important, too.

CONNECTIVITY PATTERNS

The Liner Shipping Connectivity Index (see box 1.2) allows for an immediate intuitive grasp of the main connectivity patterns in the Mediterranean. Its dataset gives evidence on the growing importance of emerging and middle-income countries in maritime networks, and the Mediterranean is seeing three categories of countries emerge among those networks. The first is countries that are global hubs or gateways because their hinterland is important or because they host a transshipment port of global importance. Most of these economies are in the west—primarily France, Italy, Malta, Morocco (which joined the group with the construction and expansion of Tanger Med), and Spain. Morocco has shown the fastest growth on the Liner Shipping Connectivity Index since 2004. Egypt is also in this group because of the Suez Canal and its associated hub.

The second category is regional gateways that have typically experienced fast growth, such as Israel and Turkey. Despite recent economic travails, Greece has also seen a connectivity boost, thanks to performance gains at Piraeus, leased to the Chinese operator COSCO.

The third category is the least connected countries, which include small economies in the Balkans and relatively large economies in North Africa such as Algeria and Tunisia (table 1.3).

TABLE 1.3 **Liner shipping connectivity index values in the Mediterranean**

COUNTRY	2004	2008	2012	2016
Global hubs or gateways				
Spain	54	68	74	86
France	67	66	70	84
Italy	58	56	66	67
Morocco	9	30	55	65
Egypt, Arab Rep.	43	53	57	63
Malta	28	30	45	58
Regional gateways				
Turkey	26	36	53	50
Portugal	18	35	46	48
Greece	30	27	46	47
Israel	20	20	31	37
Lebanon	11	29	43	35
Slovenia	14	16	22	33
Croatia	9	15	21	33
Least-connected Mediterranean countries				
Cyprus	14	12	16	19
Syrian Arab Republic	9	13	16	13
Algeria	10	8	8	6
Tunisia	9	7	6	5
Libya	5	5	8	5
Albania	0	2	1	3
Montenegro	3	3	1	3
Global benchmarks				
China	100	137	156	167
Singapore	82	94	113	123
Netherlands	79	88	89	96

Source: Calculation based on data from the United Nations Conference on Trade and Development's UNCTADstat database (http://unctadstat.unctad.org/wds/TableViewer/tableView.aspx?ReportId=92).
Note: Index, 100 = China in 2004. Higher values indicate better connectivity.

ANNEX 1A: POTENTIAL INDICATORS AT THE COUNTRY AND PORT LEVELS

TABLE 1A.1 **Full menu of port performance indicators, with country- and port-level indicators**

INDICATOR TOPIC	COUNTRY-LEVEL		PORT-LEVEL	
	INDICATOR	DATA AVAILABLE?	INDICATOR	DATA AVAILABLE?
Connectivity indicators				
Containers	Liner Shipping Connectivity Index	Yes, at http://unctadstat.unctad.org/wds/TableViewer/tableView.aspx?ReportId=92	Connectivity indicator based on ship schedules or ship movement data	Subject to agreement with data provider (Lloyd's List Intelligence, https://lloydslist.maritimeintelligence.informa.com; Alphaliner, https://www.alphaliner.com)
Roll-on, roll-off	—	—	Connectivity indicator based on ship schedules	Secondary data collection sourced from publicly available data from shipping companies is generally feasible
Intermodal connectivity	—	—	Connectivity indicator based on data from rail operators or port authority	Requires substantial effort, generally through contact with port authority and rail operators at each port
Governance indicators				
Quality of customs	World Bank quality of customs indicator	Yes, at https://data.worldbank.org/indicator/LP.LPI.CUST.XQ	—	—
Private sector participation	—	—	Private sector participation in terminal operations	Secondary data collection sourced from publicly available data (mainly websites of the companies that operate terminals)
Corporatization	—	—	Whether government-owned port authority has been corporatized	Secondary data collection sourced from publicly available data from port authorities.
Logistics	—	—	Whether there is a logistics zone in the (vicinity of) port complex	Secondary data collection sourced from publicly available data from investment promotion agencies
Corridor governance	—	—	Whether there is a corridor governance structure in the largest corridor	Secondary data collection sourced from publicly available data about corridors; definitional issues need to be addressed
Terminal operations and productivity indicators				
Quality of ports infrastructure	World Economic Forum indicator on quality of ports infrastructure	Yes, at https://data.worldbank.org/indicator/IQ.WEF.PORT.XQ	—	—
Container volume			Total throughput of the port	Subject to agreement with or purchase from IHS Markit (https://ihsmarkit.com); generally available from port authority or national statistics agency.

(continued)

TABLE 1A.1, *Continued*

INDICATOR TOPIC	COUNTRY-LEVEL		PORT-LEVEL	
	INDICATOR	DATA AVAILABLE?	INDICATOR	DATA AVAILABLE?
Container terminal productivity	—	—	*Journal of Commerce* indicator on container terminal productivity	Subject to agreement with *Journal of Commerce* (https://www.joc.com/special-topics/port-productivity)
Container dwell times	—	—	Container dwell times at terminal	Yes, but requires substantial effort per port; there are data confidentiality issues
Congestion indicators				
Road	World Economic Forum indicator on quality of roads infrastructure	Yes, at http://reports.weforum.org/global-competitiveness-index/competitiveness-rankings/	Road congestion indicator	Secondary data collection sourced from publicly available data are generally feasible, subject to coverage of the port (for instance, Waze covers most developed economies but has limited data for developing economies).
Sea	—	—	Maritime congestion indicator	An indicator can be developed based on Automatic Identification System[a] data; a third-party indicator (based on Marine Traffic data) is under development

Source: Based on the experiences with port performance measurement by PORTOPIA, a research project funded by the European Union (see www.portopia.eu).
Note: For a general approach, country- and port-level indicators are complementary. Port-level data are richer because they are more disaggregated, but country-level indicators allow for analysis alongside other country-level statistics (trade, ease of doing business, logistics performance, economic development, and so on); — = not available.
a. A global positioning satellite–based system of location for vessels that helps authorities managed the traffic in their areas of control.

NOTES

1. Ports may also serve as intermediate hubs for cargo that arrives and leaves by sea—containers, liquids, and dry bulk. The distinction between hub traffic and gateway traffic is important but blurred in practice. Take the example of Zeebrugge: a container that arrives there and leaves for the United Kingdom on a feeder vessel would be part of the hub function. In contrast, a container that leaves for the United Kingdom by train or ferry, either on a truck or on a trailer, would be part of the gateway function. Notwithstanding these definitional issues, this chapter uses the common definition of the port hinterland as the area to and from which freight moves by truck, train, or inland barge.
2. The term comes from the German word for "land behind."
3. See www.ufmsecretariat.org for more information.
4. As one example, while dwell time (of transit containers) is a huge issue in Africa, it is far less of an issue in Europe, given the more harmonized and streamlined customs procedures.
5. The remaining analysis focuses on trains because the number of ports with high inland barge traffic is very limited. Of the identified EU core ports, less than 5 percent have container barge services.
6. More complicated indicators would attribute a link quality to each link and then sum the link qualities of all unique destinations.
7. This is not a black or white distinction: port authorities can have some but not full autonomy. The analysis draws on the composition of the supervisory board (if any), hiring practices of the port authorities, and their commercial freedom to negotiate prices.

8. There is much more to institutions, however. For instance, the above corridors often require active forms of governance or management, though cooperative platforms and project-by-project cooperation efforts can work well. Thus there is no emerging best model that reduces the value of inclusion of such information in a dashboard. Still, in some contexts (especially in Africa, with corridors to landlocked countries) such an indicator is useful.

REFERENCES

Arvis, J.-F., Y. Duval, B. Shepherd, and C. Utoktham. 2013. "Trade Costs in the Developing World: 1995–2010." Policy Research Working Paper 6309, World Bank, Washington, DC.

Arvis, J.-F., and B. Shepherd. 2011. "The Air Connectivity Index: Measuring Integration in the Global Air Transport Network." Policy Research Working Paper 5722, World Bank, Washington, DC.

Cheon, S., D. E. Dowall, and D. W. Song. 2010. "Evaluating Impacts of Institutional Reforms on Port Efficiency Changes: Ownership, Corporate Structure, and Total Factor Productivity Changes of World Container Ports." *Transportation Research Part E: Logistics and Transportation Review* 46 (4): 546–61.

Commission of the European Communities. 2001. "European Transport Policy for 2010: Time to Decide." European Commission. Brussels.

De Langen, P. W., and C. Heij. 2014. "Corporatisation and Performance: A Literature Review and an Analysis of the Performance Effects of the Corporatisation of Port of Rotterdam Authority." *Transport Reviews* 34 (3): 396–414.

Eurostat. 2017. "Maritime Transport Statistics—Short Sea Shipping of Goods." Luxembourg. http://ec.europa.eu/eurostat/statistics-explained/index.php/Maritime_transport_statistics_-_short_sea_shipping_of_goods.

Fremont, A. 2007. "Global Maritime Networks: The Case of Maersk." *Journal of Transport Geography* 15 (6): 431–42.

Hoffman, J. 2005. "Liner Shipping Connectivity." *UNCTAD Transport Newsletter* 27 (1): 4–12.

Jiang, J., L. H. Lee, E.P. Chew, and C.C. Gan. 2015. "Port Connectivity Study: An Analysis Framework from a Global Container Liner Shipping Network Perspective." *Transportation Research Part E: Logistics and Transportation Review* 73: 47–64.

Kunaka, C., and Carruthers, R. 2014. *Trade and Transport Corridor Management Toolkit*. World Bank. Washington, DC.

Maersk. 2014. "A Leading Trade Nation: The Role of Container Shipping and Logistics in Enhancing Trade and Economic Growth in China." Copenhagen. https://www.maersk.com/-/media/business/sustainability/china-impact-study.ashx.

Ojala, L., and J. Hoffman. 2010. "A Comparison of the LPI and the LSCI." *Transport Newsletter* 46: 7–8.

Rodrigue, J.-P. 2012. "The Geography of Global Supply Chains: Evidence from Third Party Logistics." *Journal of Supply Chain Management* 48 (3): 15–23.

Rodrigue, J.-P., C. Comtois, and B. Slack. 2017. *The Geography of Transport Systems*. 4th ed. New York: Routledge.

Rodrigue, J-P and T. Notteboom (2010) "Foreland-Based Regionalization: Integrating Intermediate Hubs with Port Hinterlands", Research in Transportation Economics, Vol. 27, pp. 19–29.

Scheidel, W., and E. Meeks. 2012. "ORBIS: The Stanford Geospatial Network Model of the Roman World." http://orbis.stanford.edu.

Tang, L.C., J.M. Low, and S.W. Lam. 2011. "Understanding Port Choice Behavior—A Network Perspective." *Networks and Spatial Economics* 11 (1): 65–82.

World Bank. 2003. *Port Reform Toolkit*. World Bank. Washington, DC.

———. 2016. *Connecting to Compete 2016: Trade Logistics in the Global Economy*. Washington, DC.

World Trade Organization. 2015. *World Trade Report 2015: Speeding up Trade*. World Trade Organization. Geneva.

2 Maritime Networks and Port Efficiency

This chapter focuses on the quantitative analysis of shipping and port dynamics taking place in the Mediterranean region over 2009–16). A complementary analysis examines major trends in recent and current patterns of maritime flows for port hierarchy and network connectivity.

THE GLOBAL CONNECTIVITY OF MEDITERRANEAN PORTS

The Mediterranean is a major shipping crossroad and key segment of the round-the-world trunk line (the optimal shipping route), yet it has its own features in its maritime forelands (that is, the distribution of overseas connectivity) because of its physical geography and long-term trading inheritance. Containerization is particularly strategic in the region, as evidenced by the increased amount of research on container shipping that has covered the Mediterranean in recent decades (Lau et al. 2017). On the basis of direct/adjacent calls with the rest of the world, Europe is by far the Mediterranean's main connection, with about 40–50 percent of total extra-Mediterranean traffic on average over the study period (figure 2.1). Since 2009, Europe's share has increased at the expense of West Asia (around 20 percent), North America, East Asia, and Africa (10 percent each). Because of its remoteness, Oceania is rarely connected by single-ship movements with the Mediterranean. On the basis of all calls, East Asia is the Mediterranean's main connection (30–40 percent), but its share has decreased relative to those of Europe (20 percent) and West Asia since 2013 (12 percent).

Port hierarchy

Ports in the Mediterranean are heterogeneous in volume and share of extra-Mediterranean traffic in total traffic (table 2C.1). On the basis of direct/adjacent calls, a few ports (Algeciras, Spain; Sines, Portugal; and Tanger Med, Morocco) combine large volume and high share thanks to their interlining function between east–west and north–south lanes (map 2.1, top panel). Other large ports (Cagliari, Italy; Damietta, the Arab republic of Egypt; Piraeus; Salerno, Italy; and Valencia,

FIGURE 2.1

Extra-Mediterranean traffic of Mediterranean ports, by region, 2009–16 (percent of total twenty-foot equivalent unit (TEU) traffic)

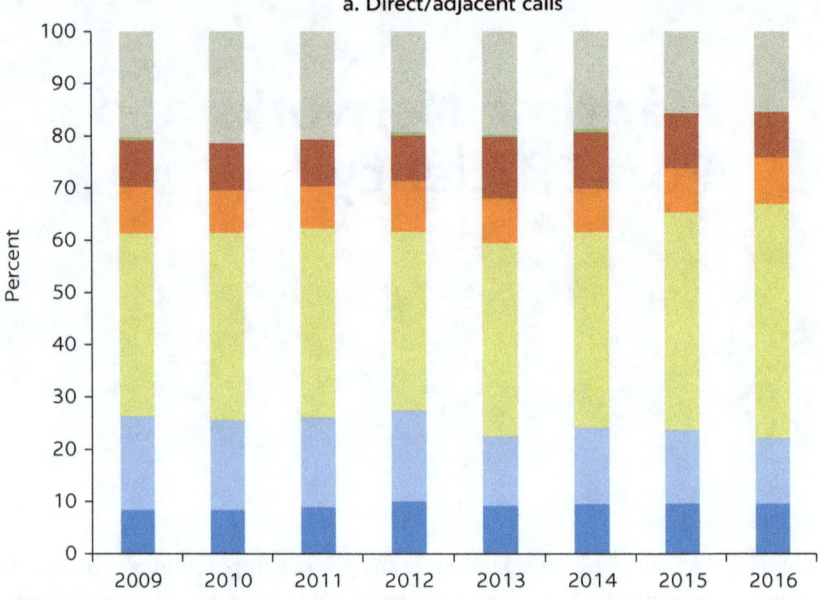

a. Direct/adjacent calls

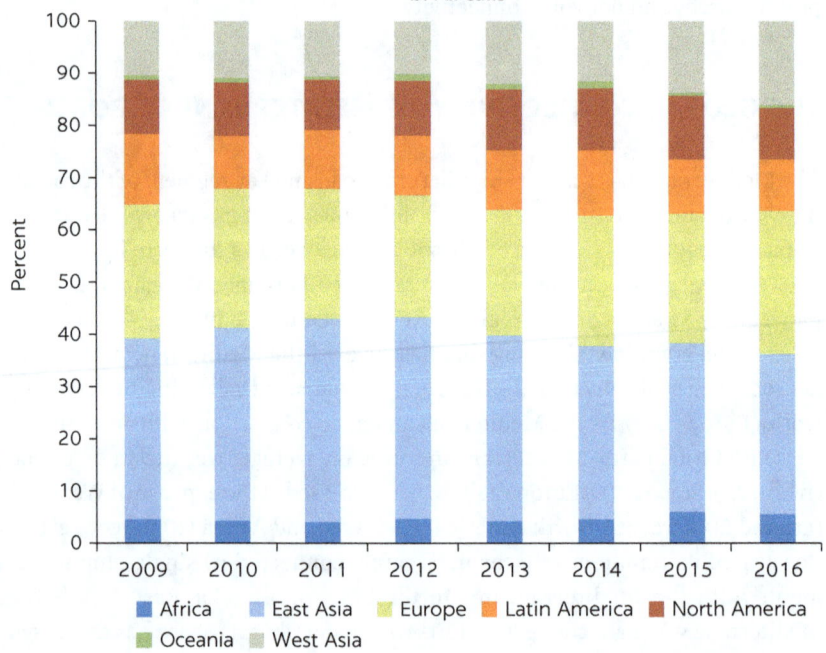

b. All calls

Source: World Bank calculations based on data from Lloyd's List Intelligence (see annex 2A).
Note: Data for 2016 cover only May and June.

MAP 2.1

Share of extra-Mediterranean traffic in total traffic at Mediterranean ports, 2015 (percent of total TEU traffic)

a. Direct/adjacent calls

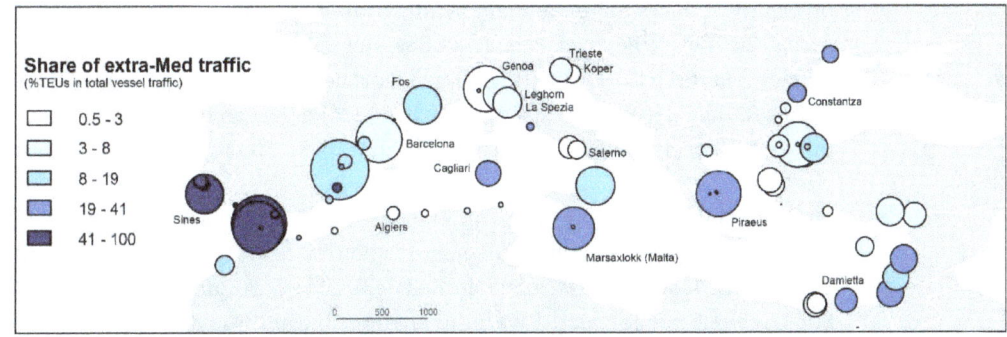

b. All calls

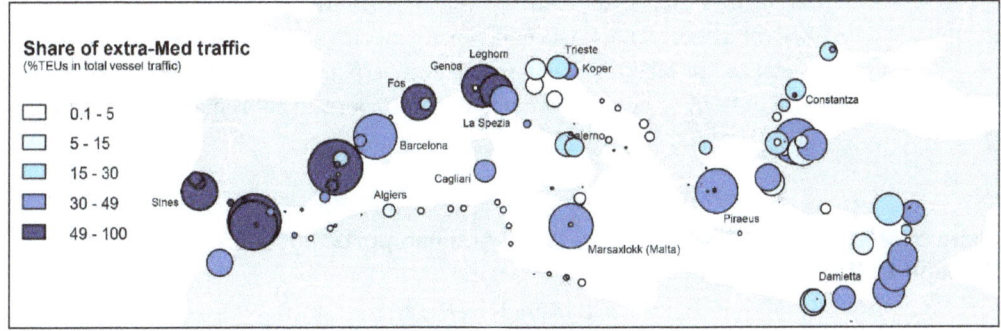

Source: Produced by Marie Metge (Centre national de la recherche scientifique) based on data from Lloyd's List Intelligence (see annex 2A).

Spain) have large shares as well (24–49 percent), close as they are to the trunk line (the optimal shipping route) between the Strait of Gibraltar and the Suez Canal. Distances from this corridor reduce the ability of other ports (Ashdod, Israel; Barcelona; Constantza, Romania; Koper, Slovenia; La Spezia, Italy; Leghorn, Italy; and Trieste, Italy), even large ones, to connect with ports outside the Mediterranean through direct vessel movements (Zohil and Prijon 1999).

The picture is similar on the basis of all calls, although the ability to connect more distant markets is spread more evenly, including hub ports (such as Gioia Tauro, Italy, and Valencia, Spain) and gateway ports (Fos [Marseilles], Genoa, and La Spezia, Italy; see map 2.1, bottom panel). Distance to the trunk line is thus compensated for by good insertion in shipping company networks that are involved in pendulum services connecting non-Mediterranean regions. A few ports remain somewhat peripheral in any case, such as those along the North African coast (except Casablanca). For example, Algiers, for which 5–15 percent of total traffic is extra-Mediterranean on the basis of all calls (0–3 percent on the basis of direct calls), connects overseas regions only indirectly, through transshipment at certain Mediterranean hubs (for example, Malta), mainly because its trade volume remains too small to attract pendulum services. Adriatic ports also have limited global connectivity.

On the basis of volume and share of intra-Mediterranean traffic in total traffic at non-Mediterranean ports by direct/adjacent calls, the busiest traffic nodes are in West and East Asia, Northern Europe, North America's East Coast, the Caribbean, and Latin America's East Coast (map 2.2, top panel). This pattern reveals the Mediterranean's function as a transshipment region between the world's main economic powerhouses (map 2.3). By share of traffic, geographic proximity appears to be the main factor, with higher shares in ports in West Africa, the Iberian Peninsula, the Black Sea, and the Red Sea. Exceptions include Canada (Halifax and Montreal) and Brazil (Fortaleza and Recife). The Hamburg–Le Havre range does not really specialize in Mediterranean traffic despite their proximity, because they connect through multiple shipping routes with ports worldwide.

On the basis of all calls, the overall pattern is similar, if accentuated in the vicinity of the Mediterranean (see map 2.2, bottom panel). Certain ports stand out, such as Jeddah and Port Sudan (Red Sea), as well as Canary Islands ports. Some regions not connected with the Mediterranean through direct/adjacent calls emerge, such as Latin America's West Coast, North America's West Coast, and Australia, but with relatively low shares of Mediterranean traffic, given the effect of distance. East Asia and North America's East Coast are more strongly specialized in Mediterranean traffic. Antwerp and Felixstowe have the highest share (around 18 percent, compared with 10 percent at Bremerhaven, Hamburg,

MAP 2.2

Share of Mediterranean traffic at non-Mediterranean ports, 2009–15 (percent of total TEU unit traffic)

a. Direct/adjacent calls

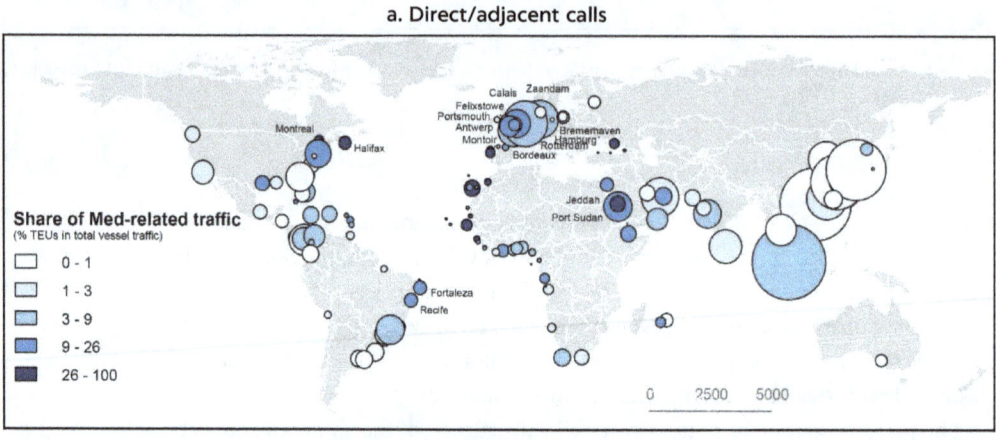

b. All calls

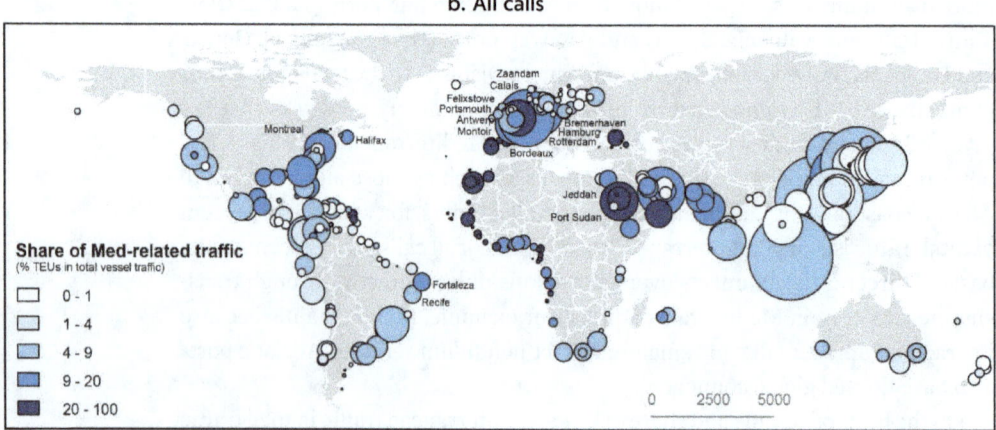

Source: Produced by Marie Metge (Centre national de la recherche scientifique) based on data from Lloyd's List Intelligence (see annex 2A).

MAP 2.3
Mediterranean and other transshipment regions

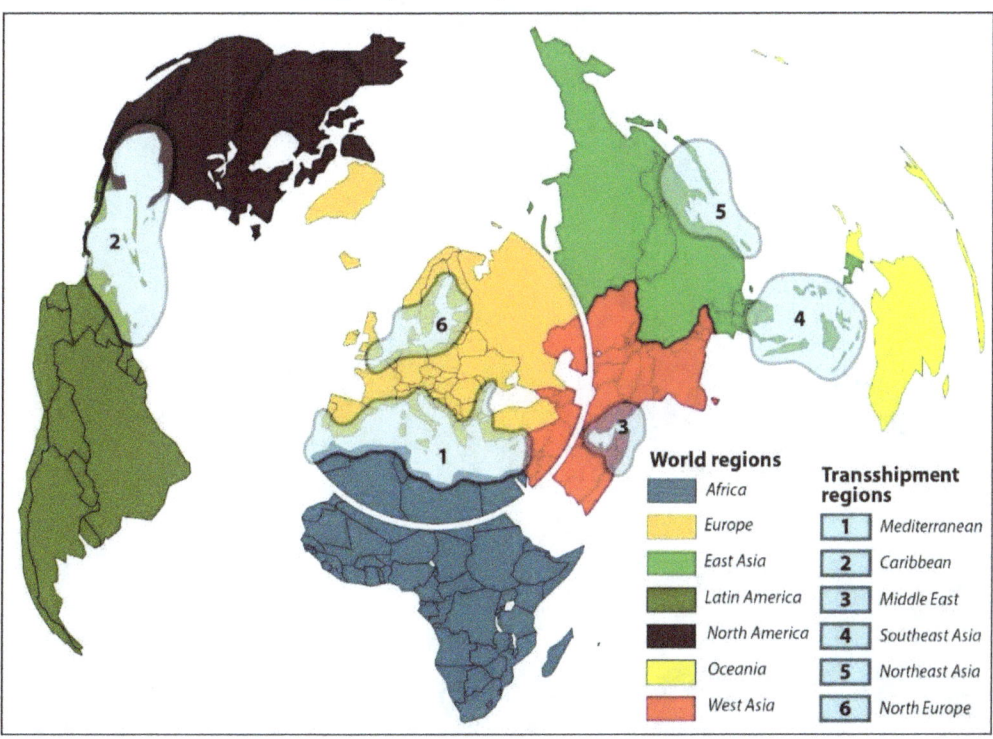

and Rotterdam), while some medium-size ports, such as Montoir (22 percent), Bordeaux (23 percent), Portsmouth (32 percent), Zaandam (64 percent), and Calais (29 percent), reflecting the continued impact of trade specialization with the Maghreb (Algeria, Libya, and Tunisia).

The top 10 Mediterranean ports by total vessel traffic can also be compared on the basis of their foreland focus, or specialization. On the basis of direct/adjacent calls, Algeciras (Spain), Marsaxlokk (Malta), and Piraeus are more focused on East Asia; Algeciras, Sines (Portugal), and Valencia (Spain) on Latin and North America; Marsaxlokk and Piraeus on West Asia; and Algeciras, Barcelona, Marsaxlokk, Tangier (Morocco), and Valencia on Africa (figure 2.2, top panel). Hub ports thus tend to be more diversified than gateway ports and to specialize in several regions. The strong specialization on Europe for other ports is the effect of distance from the trunk line. On the basis of all calls, foreland specialization is less apparent, because all major ports specialize similarly in East Asia, Europe, and North America (figure 2.2, bottom panel). Piraeus depends the most on East Asia among the top ports, perhaps an effect of COSCO's recent investments.

Global and local players

The location strategies (or port networks) of ocean shipping companies have been well studied, especially in the container business, looking at the evolving geographic coverage of major firms such as CMA CGM (Frémont 2015), COSCO and Evergreen (Comtois and Wang 2003; Rimmer and Comtois 2005), and Maersk (Frémont 2007) and large shipping alliances (McCalla, Slack,

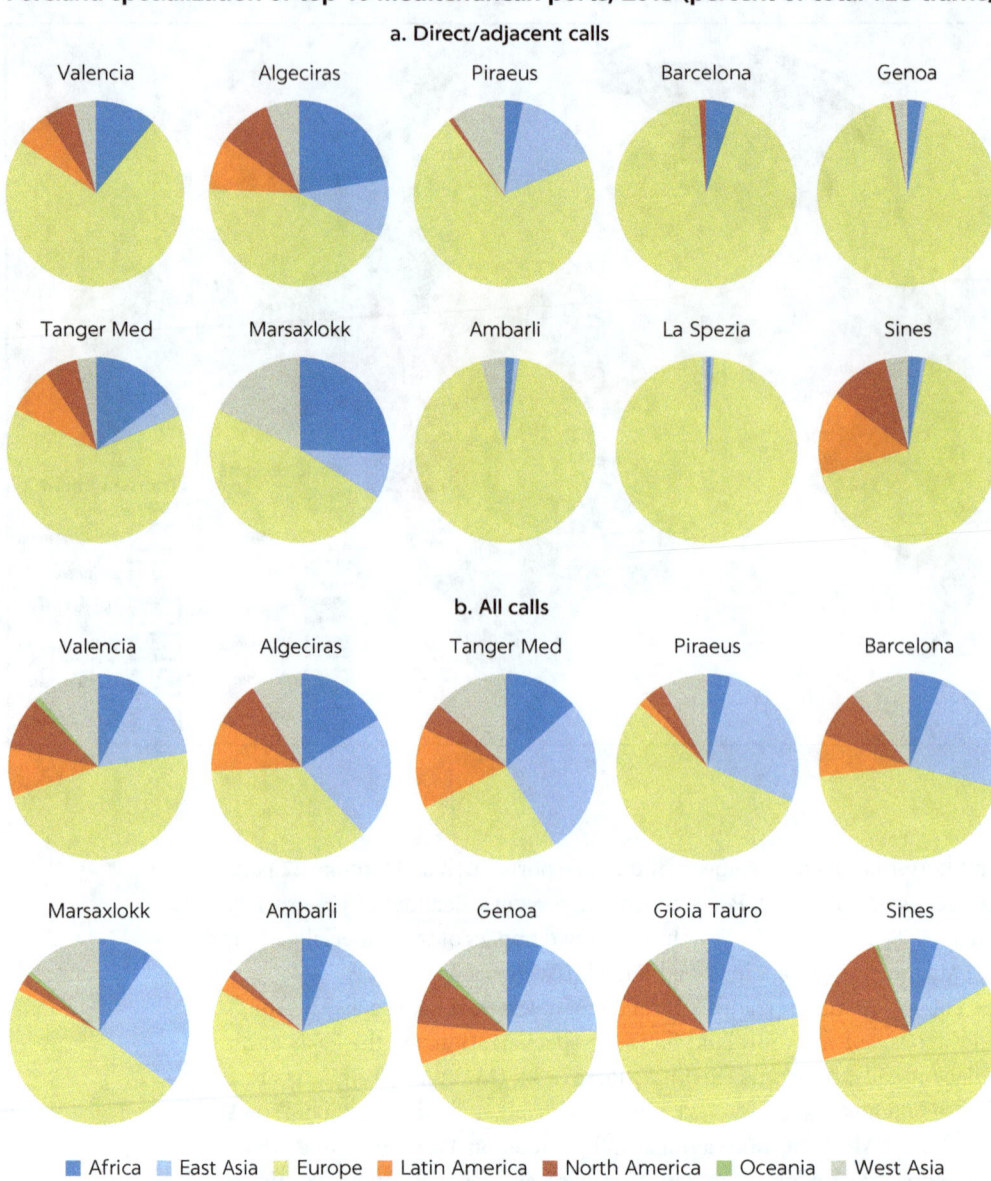

FIGURE 2.2
Foreland specialization of top 10 Mediterranean ports, 2015 (percent of total TEU traffic)

Source: World Bank calculations based on data from Lloyd's List Intelligence (see annex 2A).

and Comtois 2004). Such strategies often focus on dedicated nodes where traffic and services are concentrated.

The volume and share of vessels operated by companies belonging to major shipping alliances are distributed mainly along the trunk line from the Strait of Gibraltar to the Suez Canal (maps 2.4 and 2.5). Ports on the trunk line often have a high share of alliance traffic (33–66 percent; Damietta, Egypt; Gioia Tauro, Italy; Marsaxlokk, Malta; Tanger Med, Morocco; and Algeciras, Spain), but some small and medium-size ports away from the trunk line (North Adriatic and Ukrainian ports and Civitavecchia, Italy) do as well.

MAP 2.4
Optimal trajectory (trunk line) with the least diversion distance

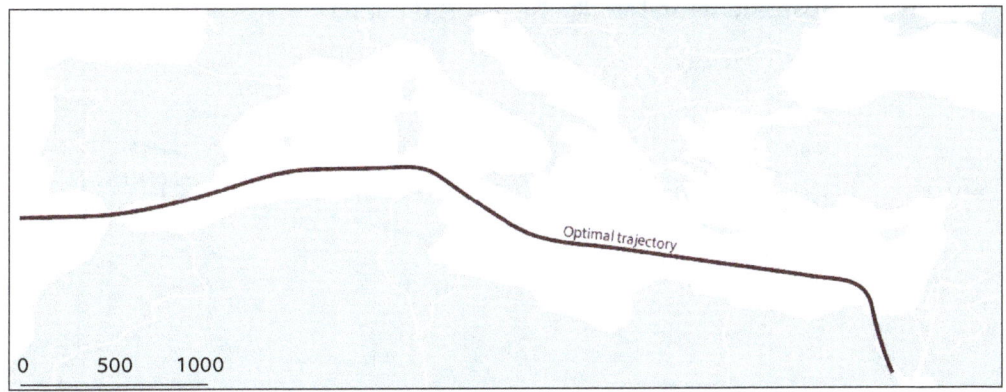

Source: World Bank based on data from Lloyd's List Intelligence. Realized by Marie Metge.

MAP 2.5
Traffic volume and share of alliance-related traffic, 2015 (percent of total TEU traffic)

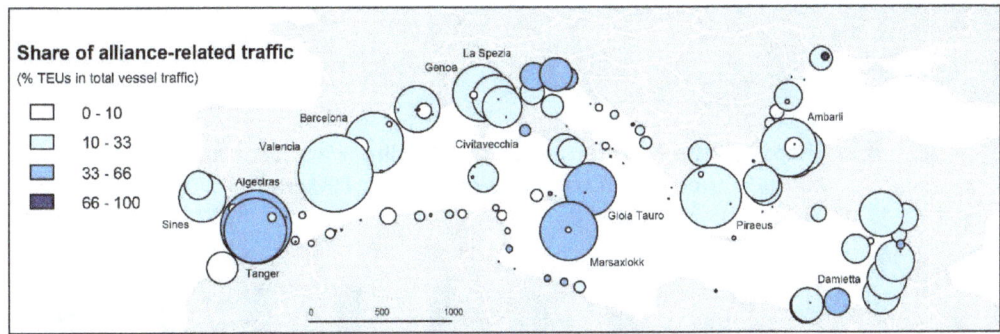

Source: Produced by Marie Metge (Centre national de la recherche scientifique) based on data from Lloyd's List Intelligence (see annex 2A).

LOCAL CONNECTIVITY OF MEDITERRANEAN PORTS

The previous section took the perspective of global connectivity of Mediterranean ports, but traffic and intraregional connections are intense. When looking at intra-Mediterranean patterns, the role of the port and connectivity patterns may differ from the global ones.

Distribution of Intra-Mediterranean traffic

Traffic distribution in the Mediterranean region grew concentrated over 2009–16, despite a slight drop in 2012–13 for ports (figure 2.3). Traffic among interport links or port pairs became more concentrated than that among ports (identified as nodes in figure 2.3), as evidenced by the increasing Gini coefficient, because the port hierarchy is relatively stable, but networks themselves have become more centralized, rationalized, and uniform (offering fewer alternatives)—as seen in the following sections. This explains why the vessel traffic share of the largest nodes, as measured by the Herfindahl-Hirschmann index,[1] has declined regularly, while the share of the largest links has increased.

FIGURE 2.3
Traffic concentration among Mediterranean nodes and links, 2009–15 (percent of total Mediterranean TEU traffic)

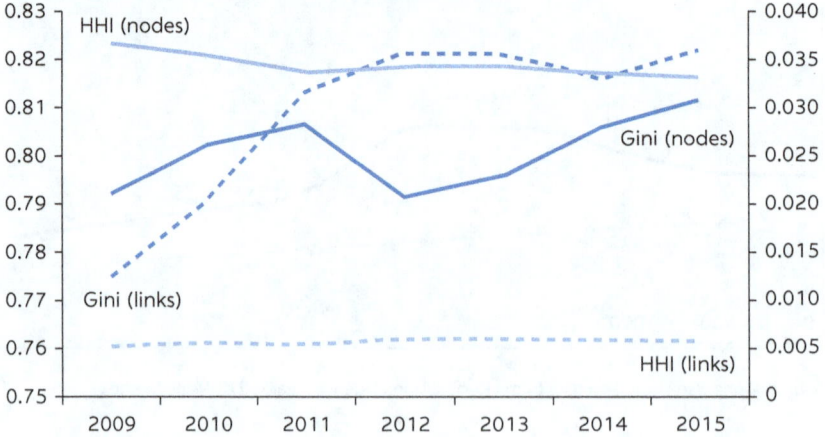

Source: World Bank calculations based on data from Lloyd's List Intelligence (see annex 2A).
Note: Both the Gini coefficient and the HHI range from 0 to 1. HHI is Herfindahl-Hirschman Index.

FIGURE 2.4
Share of intra-Mediterranean traffic, direct/adjacent and all calls, 2009–16 (percent of total Mediterranean TEU traffic)

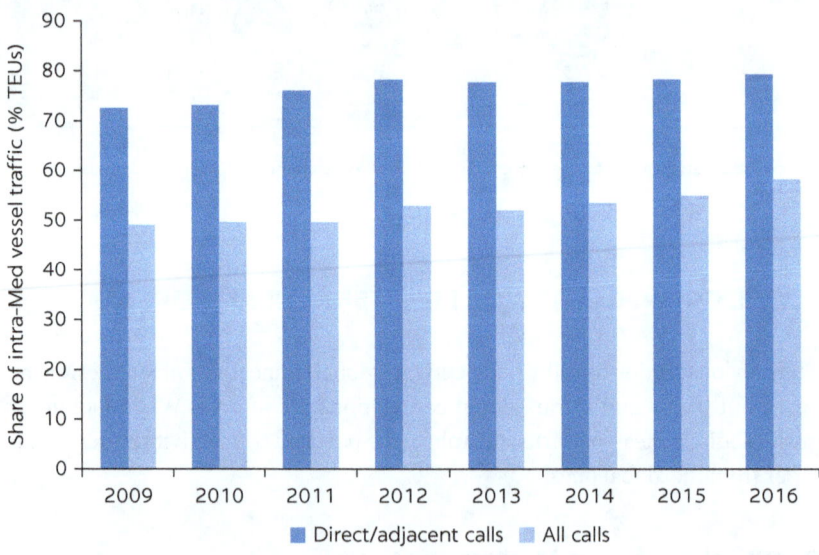

Source: World Bank calculations based on data from Lloyd's List Intelligence (see annex 2A).
Note: Data for 2016 cover only May and June.

The share of intra-Mediterranean traffic in total Mediterranean traffic—all links included—rose from 49 percent in 2009 to about 58 percent in 2016 (figure 2.4). That increase was attributable to either transshipment growth or coastal or short-sea growth. Regional integration processes as well as transit trade effects are difficult to untangle. The share based on direct/adjacent calls remained very high, increasing from 72 percent in 2009 to 79 percent

FIGURE 2.5
Intra-Mediterranean traffic distribution by subregional maritime range, all calls, 2009–16 (percent of total TEU traffic)

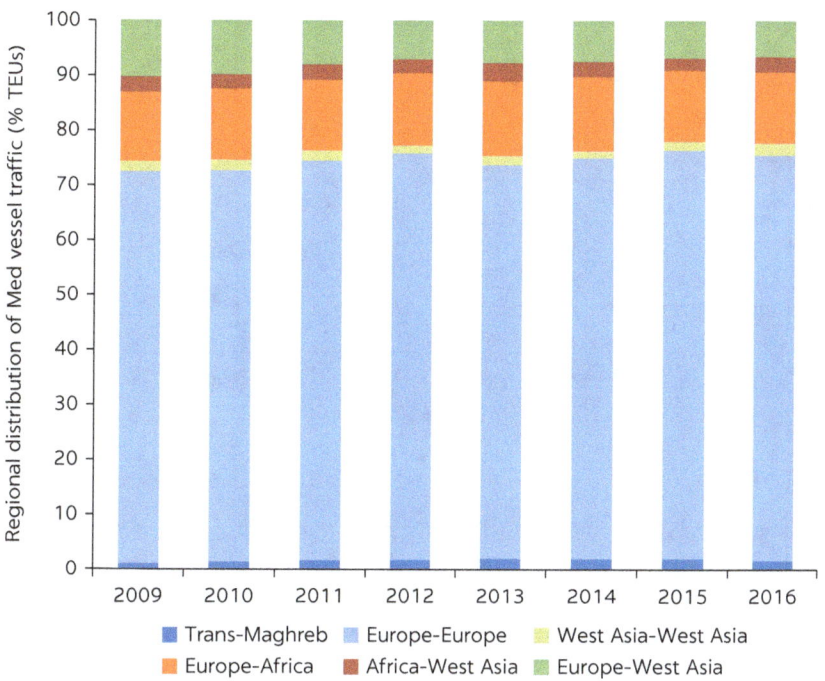

Source: World Bank calculations based on data from Lloyd's List Intelligence (see annex 2A).
Note: Data for 2016 cover only May and June; Med. = Mediterranean.

in 2016. Three main factors may explain these shifts. First, economic difficulties after the 2008–09 global financial crisis affected the degree of internationalization, as reflected in the slow growth in global connectivity (as measured by share of extra-Mediterranean traffic as a whole). Second, transshipment growth—and, notably, hub-and-spoke systems—gradually reinforced their influence. Third, increasing regionalization or regional integration fostered more short-sea shipping, backed partly by European transport policies (for example, Motorways of the Sea) and increased cross-border trade (intra-Maghreb, for example).

More than 70 percent of intra-Mediterranean traffic is intra-European, nearly 15 percent is Europe–Africa (or north–south), and less than 10 percent is Europe–West Asia traffic (figure 2.5). This pattern is reinforced by main transshipment hubs in Europe (notably in Cyprus, Greece, Italy, and Spain). Other connections lag far behind, but there has been a notable increase in trans-Maghreb traffic in recent years.

Growth of the Mediterranean networks

Throughout the Mediterranean, liner shipping is highly selective: it connects 165 of the 752 ports registered by Lloyd's List Intelligence. The decrease in the number of links based on direct/adjacent calls through 2015 suggests that companies are rationalizing routes (table 2.1). The share of redundant links (that is, those being realized in both directions, A–B and B–A) increased, pointing to the

TABLE 2.1 **Mediterranean network patterns, 2009–16**

INDICATOR	2009	2010	2011	2012	2013	2014	2015	2016[a]
Direct/adjacent calls								
Number of interport links	2,279	2,278	2,168	2,145	2,046	2,073	2,084	1,532
Number of single-way interport links[b]	1,473	1,489	1,443	1,439	1,363	1,392	1,423	1,048
Number of nodes	149	160	170	160	160	170	173	141
Density (gamma index; lower values suggest less density)	0.134	0.117	0.100	0.113	0.107	0.097	0.096	0.106
Redundant links (percent of two-way interport links)	64.6	65.4	66.6	67.1	66.6	67.1	68.3	68.4
Clustering coefficient, links (lower values suggest more hub-and-spoke structures)	0.786	0.778	0.774	0.767	0.772	0.755	0.752	0.746
Clustering coefficient, nodes (lower values suggest more hub-and-spoke structures)	0.471	0.519	0.487	0.528	0.544	0.500	0.510	0.534
Average eccentricity (lower values suggest a poorly connected network)	0.621	0.718	0.735	0.739	0.641	0.744	0.594	0.624
Average shortest path length	2.254	2.271	2.429	2.323	2.348	2.479	2.357	2.314
Centralization (degree of distribution; more-negative values suggest higher centrality)	−0.590	−0.600	−0.650	−0.682	−0.598	−0.698	−0.650	−0.714
Diameter (lower values suggest that it is easier to reach one node from another)	5	5	7	6	5	6	5	5
All calls								
Number of links	3,955	4,190	4,635	4,547	3,960	4,511	4,823	2,918
Number of nodes	154	175	175	164	165	173	177	143
Share of direct links (%)	37.2	35.5	31.1	31.6	34.4	30.9	29.5	35.9
Density (Gamma index; lower values suggest less density)	0.336	0.275	0.304	0.340	0.293	0.303	0.310	0.287
Clustering coefficient, links (lower values suggest more hub-and-spoke structures)	0.863	0.836	0.838	0.849	0.830	0.850	0.849	0.849
Clustering coefficient, nodes (lower values suggest more hub-and-spoke structures)	0.790	0.778	0.793	0.788	0.797	0.776	0.761	0.752
Average eccentricity (lower values suggest a poorly connected network)	0.569	0.708	0.649	0.595	0.530	0.568	0.600	0.564
Average shortest path length	1.700	1.778	1.727	1.678	1.753	1.747	1.737	1.788
Diameter	3	4	3	3	3	3	3	3

Source: World Bank calculations based on data from Lloyd's List Intelligence (see annex 2A).
Note: See annex 2B for definitions of the network measures.
a. Data cover only May and June.
b. Single-way interport links refer to links that go in only one direction, such as Genoa-Fos but not Fos-Genoa. The proportion of single-way interport links among the total number of links reveals the diversity or homogeneity of maritime circulations.

emergence of corridors and to mergers and alliances in the shipping sector, as the smaller number of companies consolidate their services along fewer routes, creating a more uniform system.

Other measures by shipping firms show increased network centralization—decreasing density (as measured by the Gamma index[2]) and clustering coefficients for links)—with companies rationalizing routes and simplifying services. These changes also reveal the growing importance of hubs. This is also confirmed by the increased skewness of the power-law line (scale-free) describing the distribution of connectivity (compared with the degree of centrality) among Mediterranean ports, despite some fluctuations.

The number of links based on all calls is far higher—and growing, despite a drop in 2013 (see table 2.1). Network density is also much higher, with about 30 percent of possible links operated on average. Density—and the clustering coefficient for links—fluctuates without a clear trend, though the decrease in the clustering coefficient for nodes also suggests growing centralization.

Port growth patterns

The slight and negative significance of the statistical relationship between the average traffic of ports in 2009–15 and the standard deviation of their yearly growth rates suggests that the Mediterranean port region is relatively well integrated (figure 2.6). But the statistical relationship remains rather weak, with an r-squared of only about 23 percent. Other port systems are less polycentric and perhaps already more integrated (for example, in North America's East Coast and Northwest Europe the coefficient may be 60 percent or even 80 percent. This means that the Mediterranean port system has yet to reach the maturity of some other systems.

Another way to understand port dynamics in the Mediterranean is to cluster ports according to the trajectory of their traffic (map 2.6),[3] based on the TrajPop software.[4] The six resulting clusters—with similar numbers of ports, except for cluster 6—point to several trends that reveal the internal diversity of Mediterranean ports:

- **Early growth and stability** (cluster 1): mainly Eastern Mediterranean ports (for example, Ambarli, Turkey; Ancona, Italy; Antalya, Turkey; Bourgas, Bulgaria; Damietta, Egypt; El Dekheila, Egypt; Piraeus, and Ploce, Croatia), which have become mature on their traffic growth recently
- **Stability** (cluster 2): mainly Western Mediterranean ports (Algeciras, Spain; Fos, France; Genoa, La Spezia, Italy; Leghorn, Italy; and Valencia, Spain) as

FIGURE 2.6
Average traffic size and standard deviation of traffic growth rates in the Mediterranean, 2009–15

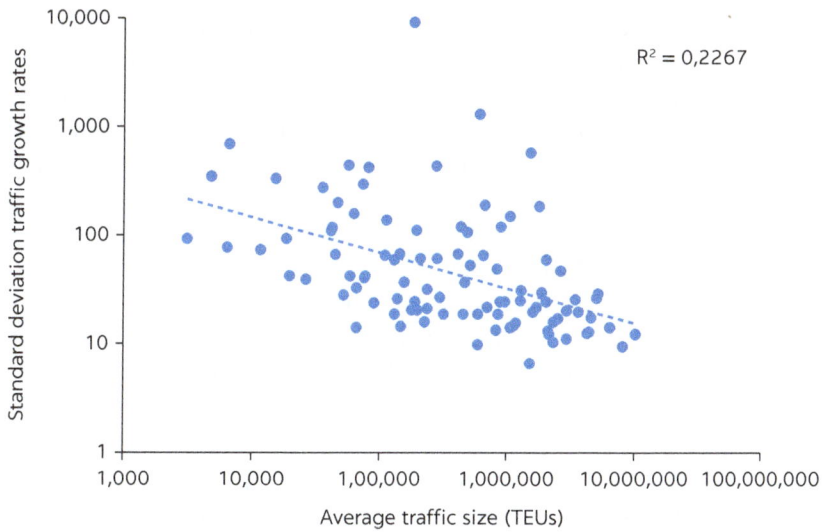

Source: World Bank calculations based on data from Lloyd's List Intelligence (see annex 2A).

MAP 2.6
Six port clusters grouped according to traffic trajectory

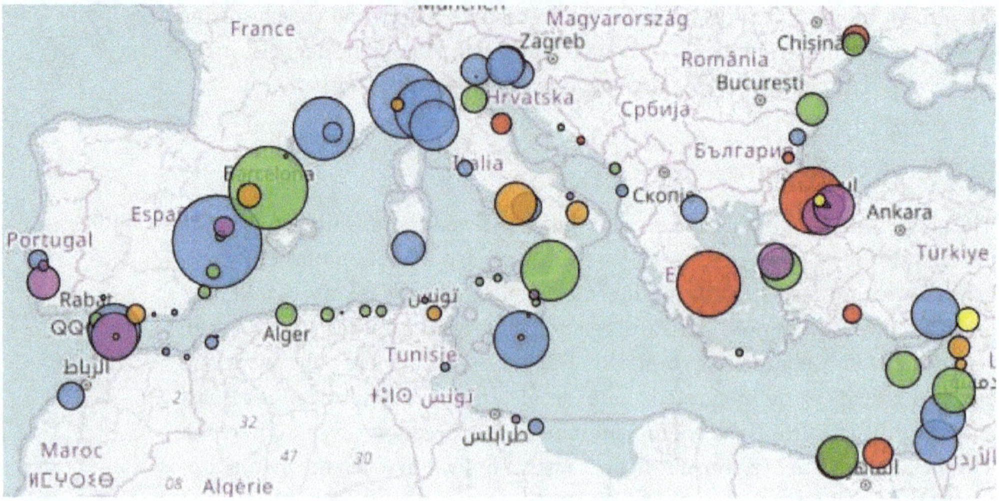

Source: World Bank calculations based on data from Lloyd's List Intelligence (see annex 2A).

well as Adriatic ports (Koper, Slovenia; Trieste, Italy; and Venice), two hubs (Cagliari, Italy; and Marsaxlokk, Malta), Eastern Mediterranean ports (Ashdod, Israel; Haifa; and Thessaloniki), Casablanca, and a few smaller ports (Civitavecchia, Italy; Durres, Albania; Lisbon; Oran, Algeria; Marseilles; Misrata, Libya; and Varna, Bulgaria)

- **Slow decline** (cluster 3): ports scattered across the Mediterranean, including large ports such as Alexandria, Beirut; Barcelona; Chornomorsk, Ukraine; Constantza, Romania; Gioia Tauro, Italy; Izmir, Turkey; and Limassol, Cyprus; and smaller ports in Algeria and southern Spain. Such ports have lost their initial importance because of port competition, traffic shifts and retention from hub ports, and unfavorable national conditions (such as inadequate policies, political tensions, economic downturns, and the like)
- **Early and fast growth** (cluster 4): mainly "strait ports" such as Evyap, Turkey; Gemlik, Turkey; Nemrut Bay, Turkey; Sines, Portugal; and Tanger Med, Morocco; but also Bari, Italy; Bizerta, Tunisia; Catania, Italy; Castellon, Spain; Ghazaouet, Algeria; Khoms, Libya; Setubal, Portugal; and Tuzla, Turkey. These ports (especially Sines and Tanger Med) quickly emerged as competitors to their neighboring hubs or as secondary ports welcoming excess traffic that could not be handled in larger, sometimes congested ports
- **Rapid decline** (cluster 5): mainly small and medium-size ports such as Lattakia, Turkey; Malaga, Spain; Naples, Radès, Tunisia; Taranto, Italy; Tarragona, Spain; and Tartous, Syrian Arab Republic, and Ceuta, Morocco; Gebze, Turkey; Pozzallo, Italy; Savona, Italy; Syros, Greece; and Valletta, Malta. The situation of these peripheral ports worsened because of increased concentration among the larger ports and hubs on which they depend as feeder ports. Container traffic is not a priority for these ports—for example, Naples is more involved in cruise and passenger shipping
- **Late and fast growth** (cluster 6): two Turkish ports, Haydarpasa and Iskenderun, quite similar to clusters 1 and 4 as defined by overall growth.

Port centrality and vulnerability to competition in maritime networks

The hub dependence index measures the share of a port's dominant traffic link in its total TEU traffic (Ducruet 2008). The higher the index value, the more a port depends on one or few connected nodes; the lower the index value, the more even the distribution of traffic. Larger ports tend to depend less on hubs than smaller ports do. Most interesting are outliers among larger ports, such as Ashdod (Israel), Evyap (Turkey), and Genoa (which have hub dependence index values of 30–40 percent (based on direct/adjacent calls) and Barcelona, Fos (France), Koper (Slovenia), La Spezia (Italy), and Leghorn (Italy) (40–60 percent). Despite bigger traffic volume, these ports have high hub dependence. There are fewer outliers when hub dependence is based on all calls—Thessaloniki, Greece (18 percent); Sfax, Tunisia (31 percent); Iraklion, Crete (38 percent); Volos, Greece (46 percent); and Sagunto, Spain (51 percent)—but the overall statistical fit is less significant. These outliers emerge because of several interrelated factors (figure 2.7):

- **Diversion distance effect:** ports situated away from the trunk line are more vulnerable to competition in maritime networks (that is, they are less attractive to mother vessels (larger vessels that make direct calls at larger hub or gateway ports) and for maritime transshipment activities, so their traffic depends largely on another port better situated along the trunk line)
- **Range effect**: well-integrated port ranges sharing multiple and common vessel calls apply to specific port groups located in close proximity along subregions such as the Western Mediterranean (Valencia, Spain–Barcelona–Fos, France–Genoa–La Spezia, Italy–Leghorn, Italy), Turkey (Evyap–Ambarli), and the North Adriatic (Venice–Koper, Slovenia–Trieste, Italy)
- **Geopolitical effect**: the dyad Ashdod–Haifa is a special case because most of Israel's trade links are with ports and regions situated outside the Mediterranean or within Israel itself
- **Hub effect**: numerous small and medium-size ports are dominated by one major hub. Yet larger ports connect to multiple hubs. For instance, Marsaxlokk (Malta) is only the third largest link of Fos (France), and although it is the dominant link of Algiers, Marsaxlokk concentrates only 16 percent of Algiers's total vessel traffic.

Single linkage analysis[5] shows that the Mediterranean port system is very polycentric—that is, organized around different poles, each with its own market area (figure 2.8). The analysis identified six subnetworks of different size (in terms of number of nodes). Regardless of whether direct/adjacent calls or all calls were considered, geographic proximity had a strong effect. Valencia (Spain) was the most central node for the Western Mediterranean, and Ambarli (Turkey) was the most central node for the Eastern Mediterranean.

Subnetworks have different topological structures—such as the chain-like Western Mediterranean subnetwork based on the range effect (France, Italy, and Spain), external hubs (Cagliari, Italy; Gioia Tauro, Italy; and Marsaxlokk, Malta), the cross-strait subnetwork of Algeciras (Spain), Sines (Portugal), and Tangier (Morocco), and the Ashdod and Haifa tandem (Israel)—because of locational (periphery) and geopolitical factors (see figure 2.8).

FIGURE 2.7

Vulnerability and traffic volume of Mediterranean ports, 2015

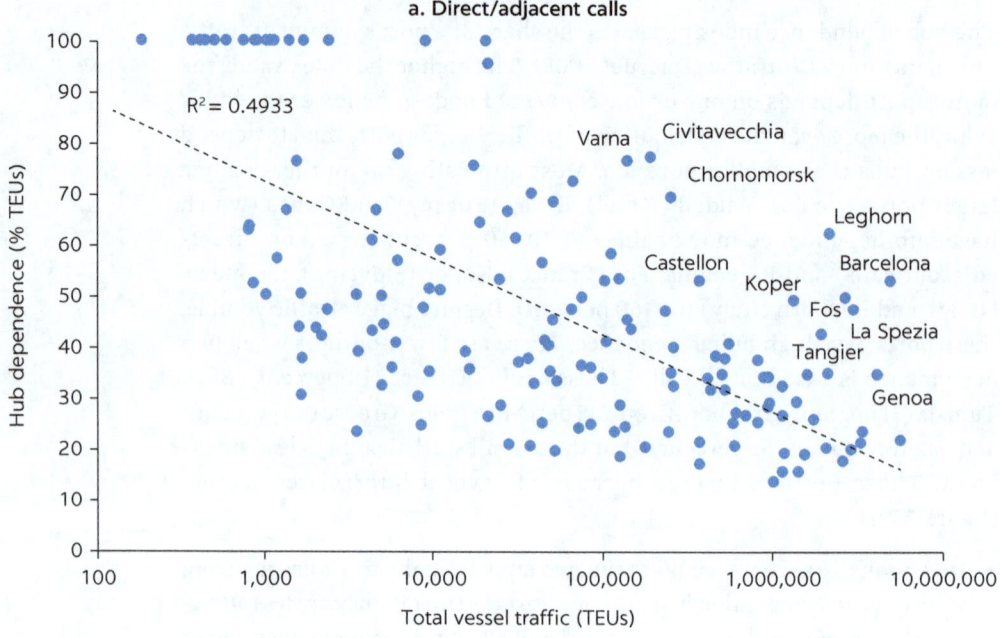

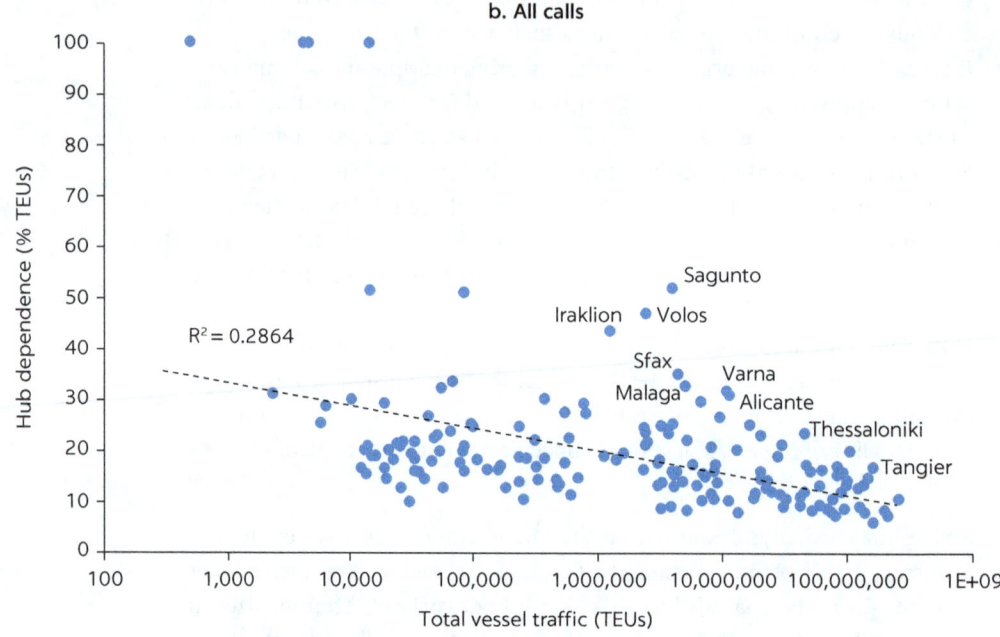

Source: World Bank calculations based on data from Lloyd's List Intelligence (see annex 2A).

More-centralized structures also emerge, such as around Ambarli (Turkey); Koper (Slovenia), and Mersin (Turkey). The specific role of Marsaxlokk (Malta) as a hub for the Maghreb appears clearly, because it is perhaps the only transshipment hub with such a dedicated catchment area in its proximity. In comparison, other transshipment hubs have a fuzzier spatial polarization (see figure 2.8).

FIGURE 2.8

Subnetworks in the Mediterranean, 2015

a. Direct/adjacent calls

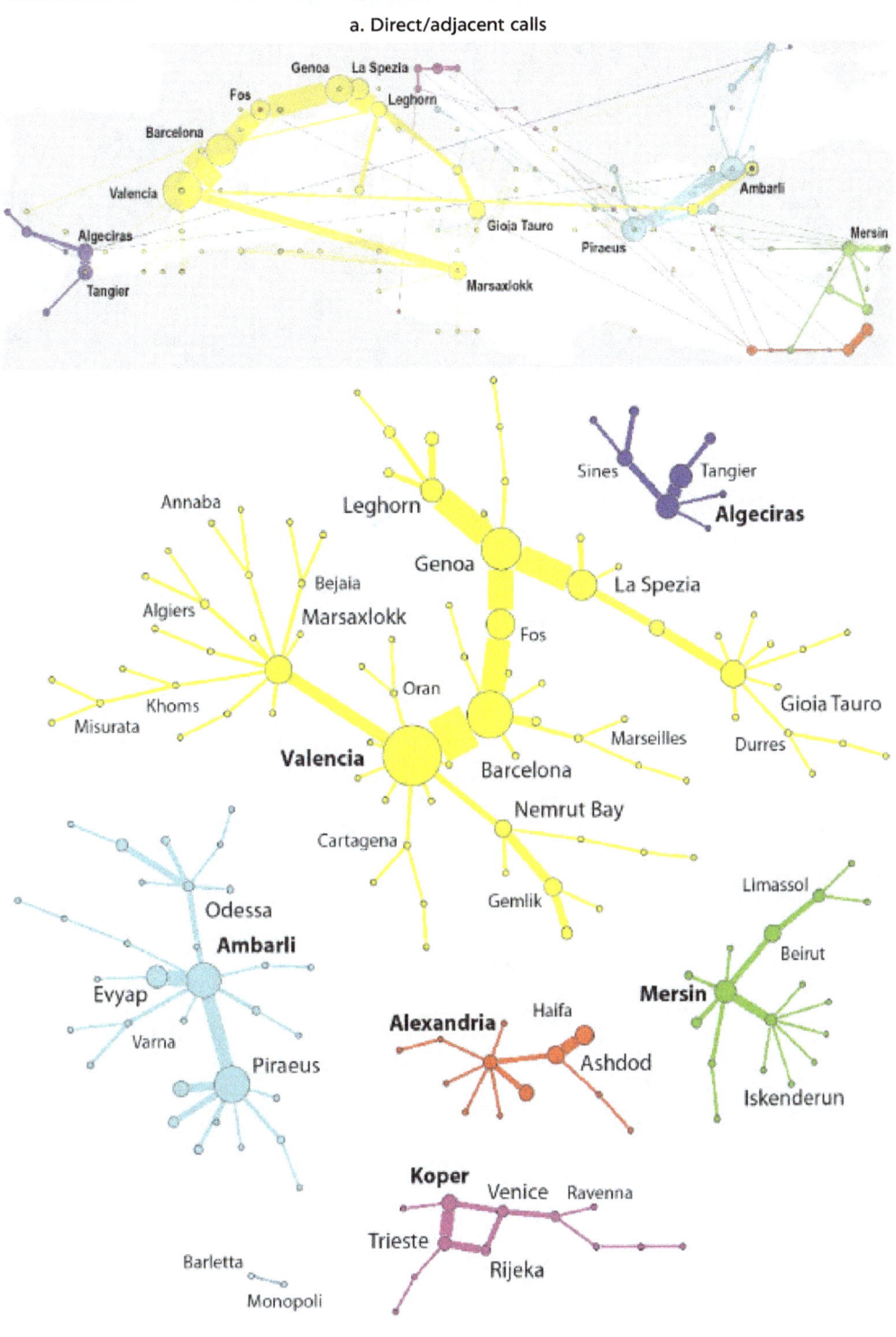

(continued)

FIGURE 2.8, *Continued*

b. All calls

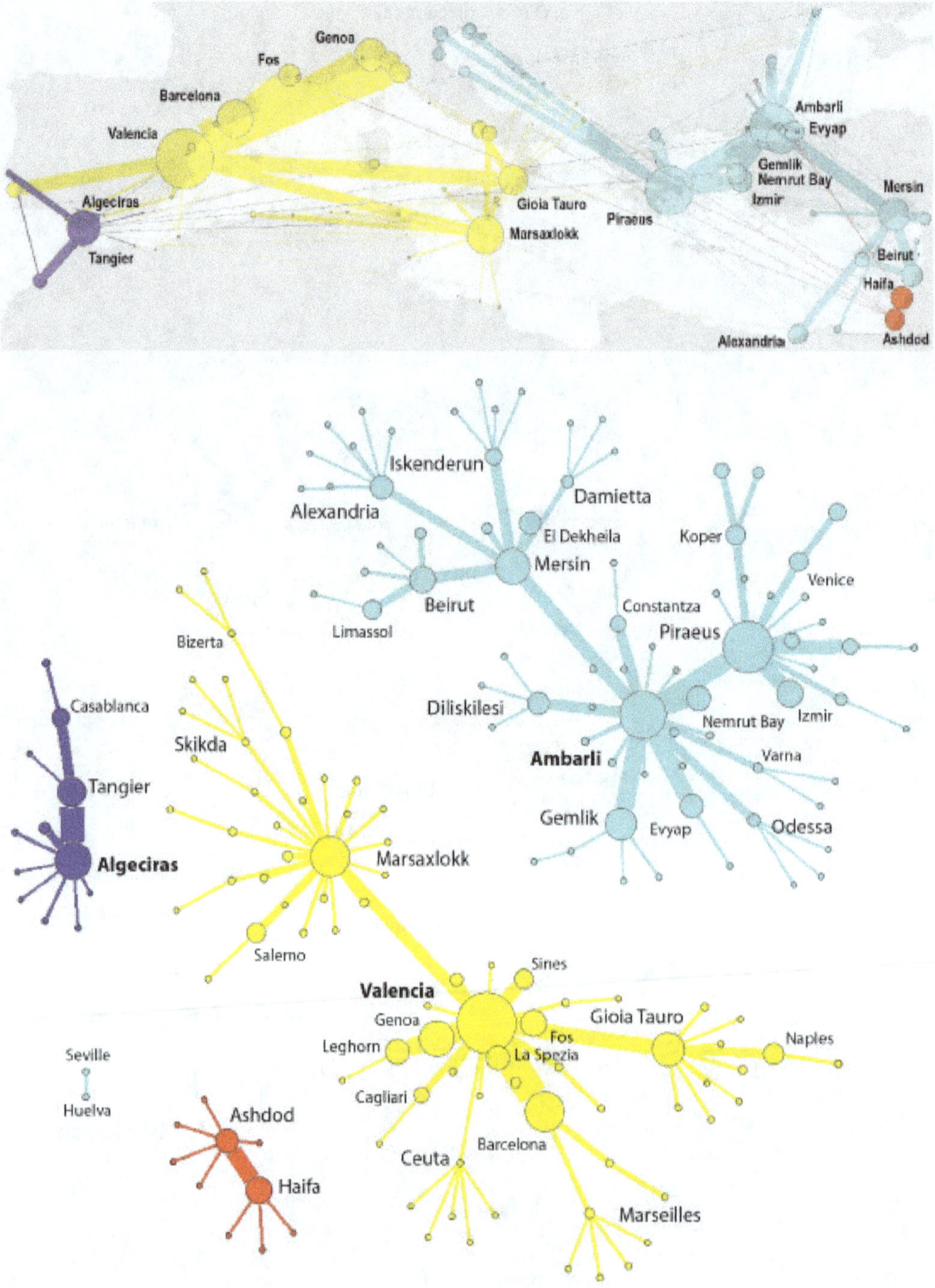

Source: World Bank calculations based on data from Lloyd's List Intelligence (see annex 2A).

Turnaround times in Mediterranean ports

The Mediterranean port system and maritime networks are regularly improving turnaround times, with both the average and standard deviation decreasing from 2009 to 2016 (figure 2.9).[6] Analysis that includes only post-Panamax-plus vessels (that is, those with a capacity of more than

8,000 TEUs) shows that larger vessels circulate faster than smaller vessels on average, despite larger vessels' (potentially) higher volumes. Port-level analysis reveals two main shifts in the average turnaround time: stability around average values (that is, around 1.5 days) and rapid improvement in time efficiency (that is, from values higher than the Mediterranean average to values lower than the Mediterranean average).

Despite the absence of a clear geographic logic, most of the long-established big ports (cluster 1, which includes Barcelona; Genoa; Piraeus; and Valencia, Spain) appear to have been stable, while many emerging ports and hub ports (cluster 2, which includes Ambarli, Turkey; Gioia Tauro, Italy; Mersin, Turkey; and Tangier, Morocco) have improved their performance (figure 2.10).

FIGURE 2.9

Vessel turnaround times in the Mediterranean for all vessels and post-Panamax-plus vessels, 2009–16 (number of days)

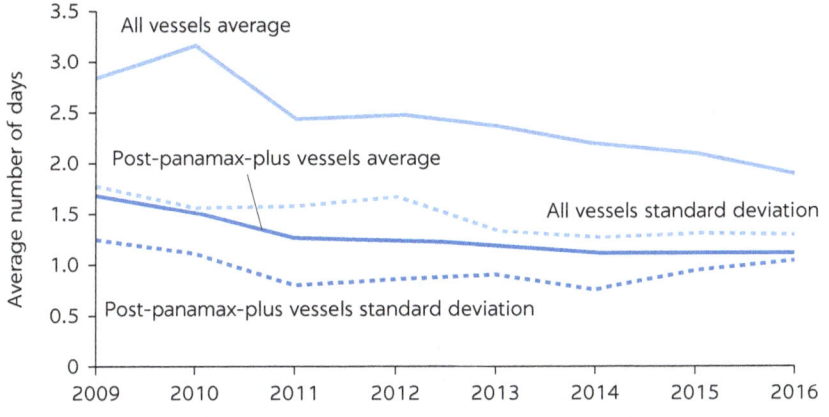

Source: World Bank calculations based on data from Lloyd's List Intelligence (see annex 2A).
Note: Data for 2016 cover only May and June.

FIGURE 2.10

Average vessel turnaround time versus number of vessel calls in the Mediterranean, 2009–16

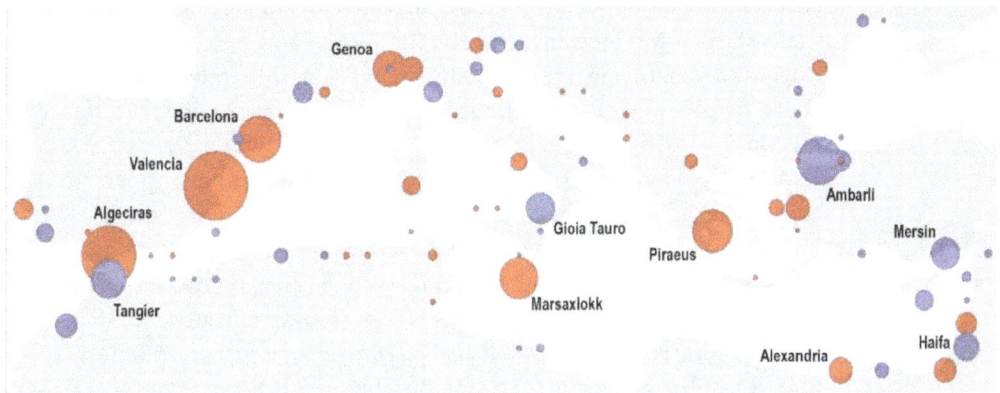

(continued)

FIGURE 2.10, continued

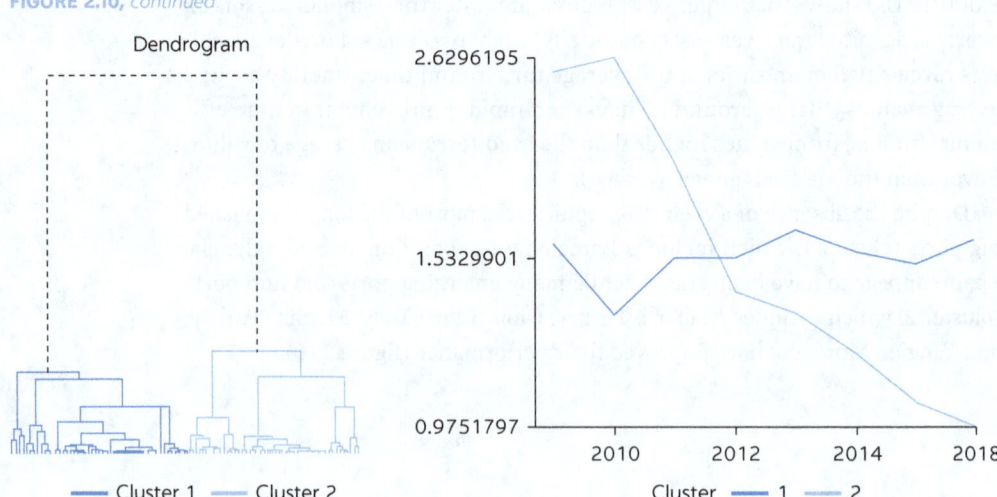

Source: World Bank calculations based on data from Lloyd's List Intelligence (see annex 2A).
Note: Data for 2016 cover only May and June.

A TYPOLOGY OF MEDITERRANEAN PORTS BY MARITIME NETWORKS AND PORT EFFICIENCY

Principal components analysis using 10 classic port performance measures and measures originating from network science[7] (on the basis of direct/adjacent calls) for 2015 for 165 Mediterranean ports shows that traffic volume and centrality go well together and do not exhibit any particular effect regardless of the type centrality considered (figure 2.11, left panel). Large ports are more central, and central ports are larger. Larger and more central ports often perform better in transit time and are closer to the trunk line. Extra-Mediterranean traffic share and alliance traffic share also stand out. The largest ports do not always attract shipping alliances but show better turnaround times, owing to the powerful position of several gateway ports in the Western Mediterranean, for instance. By contrast, being well connected outside the Mediterranean is dictated more directly by an optimal situation in the region (along the trunk line) but does not necessarily derive from shipping alliances.

Algeciras (Spain), Cagliari (Italy), Damietta (Egypt), Marsaxlokk (Malta), Sines (Portugal), and Tangier (Morocco) are the largest and most central ports and are better located but less attractive to alliances and have a higher share of extra-Mediterranean traffic (figures 2.1 and 2.5). Ambarli (Turkey), Koper (Slovenia), and Trieste (Italy) are more peripheral but have a higher share of alliance traffic, though their role is more local (a gateway function).

A comparison of the centrality of Mediterranean ports at the Mediterranean and global levels based on degree centrality (the number of links to adjacently connected ports) and betweenness centrality (number of shortest paths connecting the port) tested whether the two levels produce perfectly proportional distributions across Mediterranean ports. If a port is strongly central globally, it will also be central locally. Very few ports seem to perform better locally than globally (figure 2.12). These outliers underline an artificial border effect—that is, ports at the edge of the (arbitrarily

FIGURE 2.11
Principal components analysis of Mediterranean ports, 2015

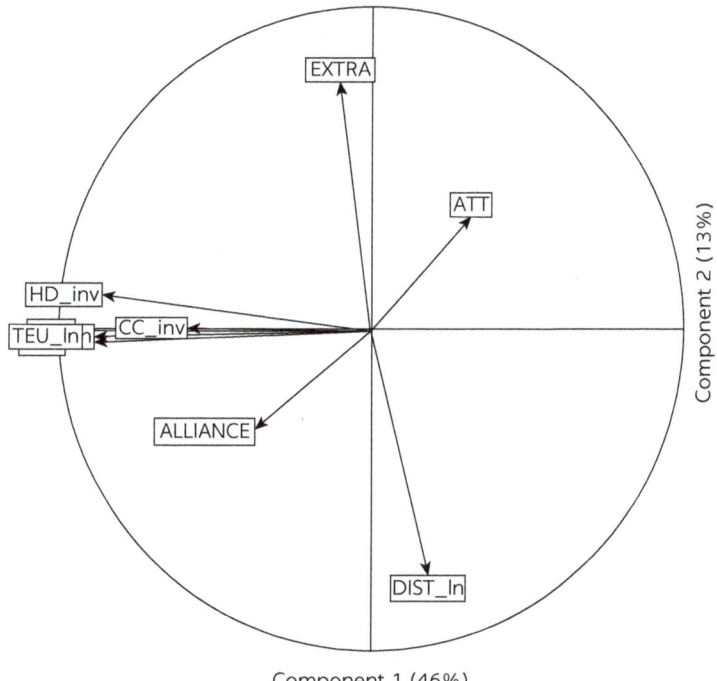

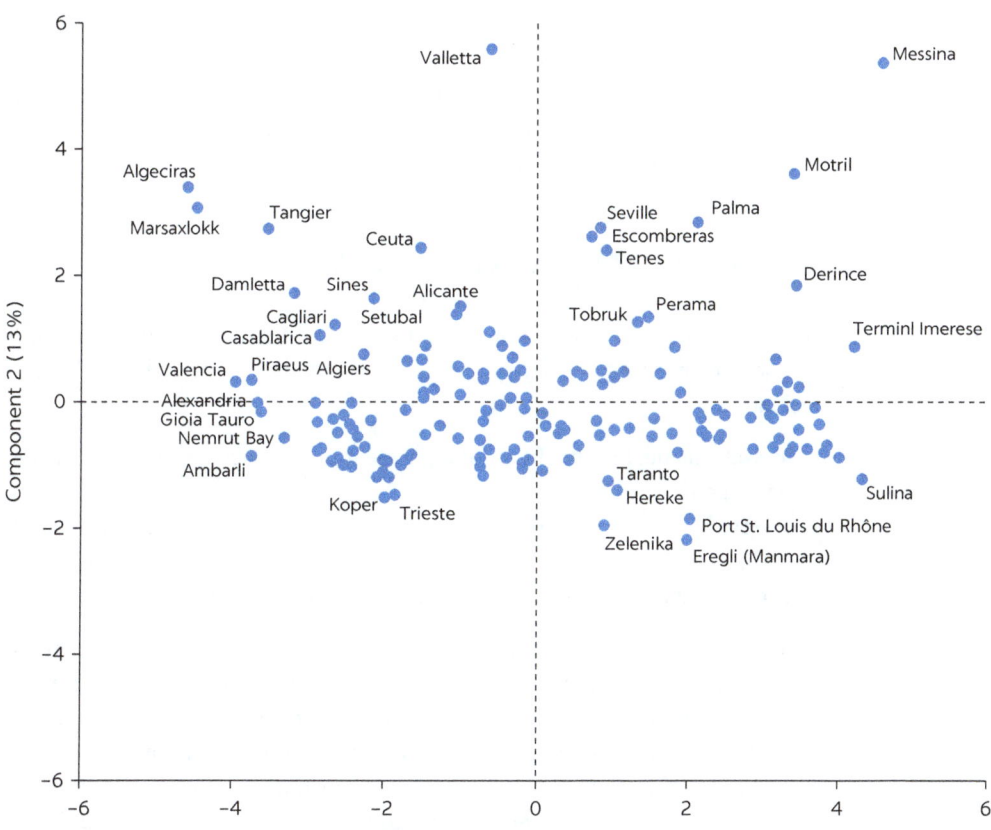

Source: World Bank calculations based on data from Lloyd's List Intelligence (see annex 2A).

FIGURE 2.12
Global versus local connectivity of Mediterranean ports, 2015

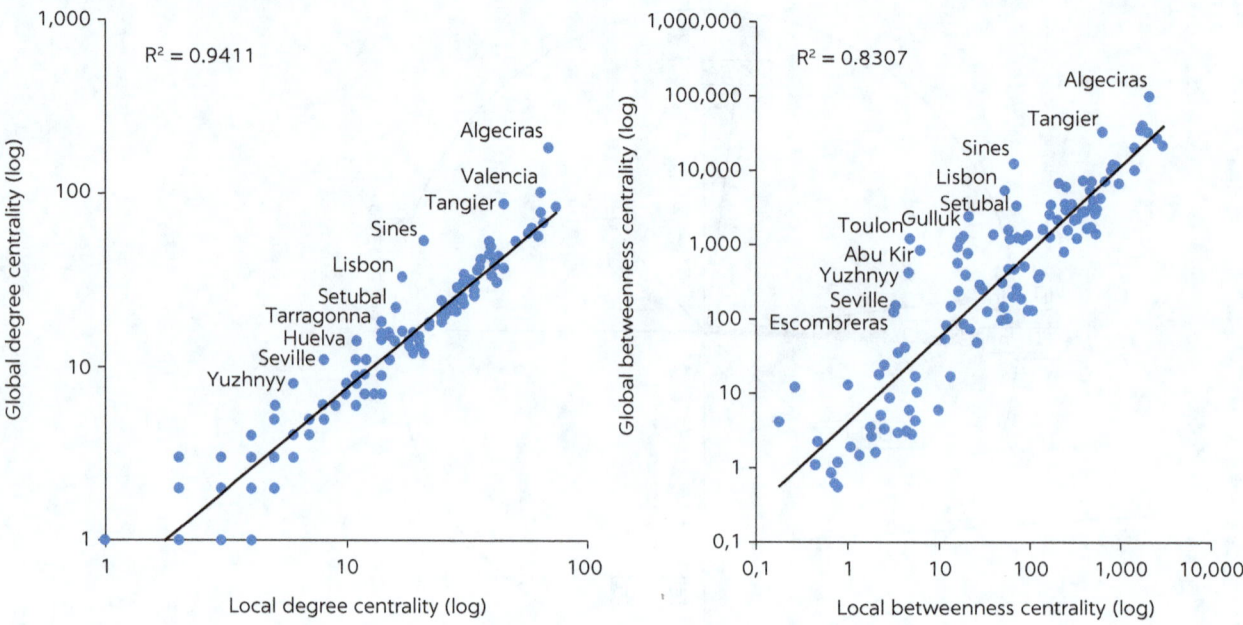

Source: World Bank calculations based on data from Lloyd's List Intelligence (see annex 2A).

defined) maritime region, such as the Strait of Gibraltar and the Black Sea, perform better globally than locally because their local centrality is not able to reflect their global centrality. The gap between local and global centrality remains a good indicator of whether a port is able to increase its connectivity beyond the sole local transport system.

ANNEX 2A: DATA AND METHODOLOGY

The data used in this chapter are from Lloyd's List Intelligence, which records the movements and successive port calls of all container ships in the world,[8] and include:

- **Vessels:** name, flag, twenty-foot equivalent unit capacity, ship operator, and date of build
- **Ports:** name, country, region, geographic coordinates, and UN location code
- **Movements:** arrival date, sailing date, and movement type.

Vessels and movements were linked through unique vessel identifications, and ports and movements were linked through unique port identifications. The data include four complete months of vessel movements (May–June and November–December) for 2009–16 and allowed for first-run basic calculations of traffic figures by port, depending on the number of vessels; the number of vessel calls; and the maximum, average, and total vessel capacity in circulation. Although several studies have used this methodology, the way the Mediterranean shipping network was constructed is also defined here (Ducruet 2015, 2017; Ducruet and Notteboom 2012).

Two network topologies correspond to an adjacency matrix with two different dimensions:

- **Direct/adjacent links**: successive port calls along the voyage of individual ships (chain). This configuration is useful to analyze hub-and-spoke systems because it gives more importance to port node neighborhood—that is, to local-level connectivity with adjacent neighbors. Because liner shipping functions through pendulum services (sometimes round the world), looking at this typology excludes the possibility for a European port to be connected to an Asian port, for instance, because the two ports lie at both ends of the service (as with node 1 and node 4 in the left panel of figure 2A.1, which are not directly connected or adjacent along the vessel's voyage)
- **All links**: all connections among ports linked by the same vessel voyage (complete graph). This configuration is useful to analyze global trade coverage and specialization of port nodes beyond their sole local environment (see the right panel of figure 2A.1). This typology allows the foreland connectivity (or overseas traffic distribution) of every port to be studied and broken down by world region, which would be impossible with the topology based on the direct/adjacent network.

Two methodological issues relate to both typologies:

- **Deletion of passage points (nonport nodes)**: passage points are included as movements in the in Lloyd's List Intelligence data but were excluded for the analysis in this chapter (with the previous and next cargo-related port calls connected in each case). Some are simple passage points between different zones (for example, Cape Finisterre and Tarifa); others are straits (for example, the Dardanelles and the Strait of Messina) or canals (the Suez Canal). Some ports are also used as passage points (for example, Gibraltar; Istanbul; Suez; and Port Said, Egypt). Although they also handle real cargo, these ports were also excluded from the analysis because the Lloyd's List Intelligence data do not always correctly specify whether ships simply pass or make a call. Including them would distort the result because they always stand out as the most central nodes and largest ports in terms of throughput.

FIGURE 2A.1

Methodology of network construction from Lloyd's List Intelligence data

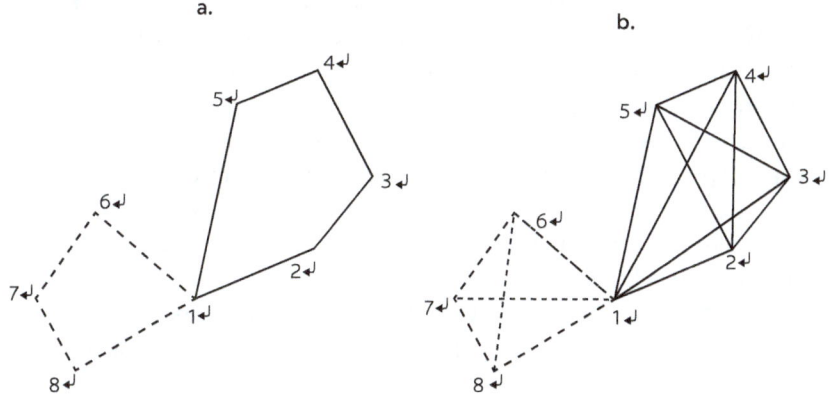

Source: Hu and Zhu 2009.
Note: Dotted lines indicate the circulation pattern of one ship, and solid lines indicate the circulation pattern of another.

- **Gap between trade routes and vessel movements**: unlike trade figures, vessel movements do not track commodities or containers themselves. This means that at many nodes the true extent of trade routes can sometimes be blurred because of transshipment operations. For example, if a port in Algeria trades with China but transfers its cargo through a hub in Malta (as CMA CGM often does), only the Algeria–Malta and Malta–China flows can be measured. Such distortions might affect understanding of the link between shipping and trade. In other words, the fact that ports are connected through vessel movements does not necessarily mean that their economies are trading with each other. If all ports belonging to the same voyage are considered to be connected (as in the right panel of figure 2A.1), the respective geographic distribution of shipping networks and origin–destination trading routes may not match—mainly because carriers need to transship at certain intermediate hubs.

ANNEX 2B: EXPLANATION OF NETWORK MEASURES

Number of links (or edges): number of relationships between ports in the network, with different numbers depending on whether directionality is taken into account (for example, Genoa–Valencia, Spain, versus Valencia–Genoa), but in general directionality of flows was excluded for simplicity. Redundant links are defined by the existence of bidirectional port pairs, as opposed to unidirectional ones.

Number of nodes (or vertices): number of ports connected in the network.

Density or completeness (Gamma index): proportion of actual links in the total maximum possible number of links among ports. Lower values suggest that the network is sparsely connected; higher values suggest a more meshed or densely connected network.

Clustering coefficient: extent to which the network is centralized. Lower values suggest the presence of hub-and-spoke structures; higher values suggest a more homogenous configuration.

Average eccentricity: topological proximity among the ports of the network. Lower values suggest a poorly connected network; higher scores suggest a well-connected network.

Average shortest path length: ease of circulation in the network—that is, the average topological length (number of links) of all the existing shortest paths in the network. Lower values suggest fewer detours and more efficient routings; higher values suggest the presence of detours and less efficient routings.

Centralization (degree of distribution): slope exponent of the power-law line obtained from the log-log distribution of the frequency of nodes along their number of connections to other ports (that is, degree centrality). Highly negative values suggest a hierarchical dimension of the network, in which a few larger nodes (high degree centrality) dominate numerous minor nodes.

Diameter: topological length of the longest path among all the shortest paths in the network. Lower values suggest that it is easier to reach one node from another; higher values suggest that it is more difficult to reach one node from another.

ANNEX 2C: TOP 20 MEDITERRANEAN PORTS BY TRAFFIC PERFORMANCE AND NETWORK CENTRALITY SCORES

TABLE 2C.1 **Total vessel traffic, 2009–16 (twenty-foot equivalent units)**

PORT	2009	PORT	2010	PORT	2011	PORT	2012	PORT	2013	PORT	2014	PORT	2015	PORT	2016[a]
Valencia (Spain)	6,998,686	Valencia (Spain)	7,420,892	Valencia (Spain)	9,281,960	Valencia (Spain)	10,693,340	Valencia (Spain)	11,224,538	Valencia (Spain)	12,380,914	Valencia (Spain)	12,592,046	Valencia (Spain)	12,540,606
Barcelona	6,175,434	Barcelona	6,920,103	Barcelona	8,028,915	Barcelona	8,470,956	Barcelona	8,191,364	Barcelona	8,882,970	Barcelona	9,658,992	Barcelona	9,385,786
Genoa	4,976,638	Genoa	5,460,229	Genoa	6,142,192	Genoa	6,477,904	Genoa	6,175,244	Genoa	6,722,932	Genoa	8,317,426	Genoa	8,924,682
Gioia Tauro	3,882,467	La Spezia	3,523,470	Ambarli (Turkey)	4,799,473	Piraeus	5,819,984	Piraeus	5,713,259	Piraeus	6,716,026	Piraeus	7,135,419	Ambarli (Turkey)	7,728,644
Fos	3,325,362	Gioia Tauro	3,346,264	Piraeus	4,359,169	Ambarli (Turkey)	5,513,382	Ambarli (Turkey)	5,604,909	Ambarli (Turkey)	6,459,557	Ambarli (Turkey)	6,790,316	Piraeus	6,445,016
La Spezia	2,877,431	Fos	3,063,232	La Spezia	4,058,504	Fos	4,975,289	Fos	5,299,387	Fos	5,814,616	Fos	5,668,012	Fos	6,037,666
Naples	2,538,400	Piraeus	2,959,516	Gioia Tauro	3,999,087	La Spezia	4,380,493	La Spezia	4,645,791	La Spezia	5,045,480	La Spezia	5,489,014	Marsaxlokk (Malta)	5,729,848
Leghorn	2,474,112	Ambarli (Turkey)	2,783,027	Fos	3,673,181	Gioia Tauro	4,176,259	Gioia Tauro	4,482,499	Gioia Tauro	4,461,653	Marsaxlokk (Malta)	5,097,976	La Spezia	5,714,128
Marsaxlokk (Malta)	2,425,428	Naples	2,530,054	Algeciras (Spain)	3,656,291	Marsaxlokk (Malta)	3,562,842	Marsaxlokk (Malta)	4,122,621	Marsaxlokk (Malta)	4,453,293	Gioia Tauro	4,868,154	Algeciras (Spain)	5,310,998
Ambarli (Turkey)	2,243,671	Marsaxlokk (Malta)	2,459,065	Leghorn	2,679,486	Algeciras (Spain)	3,505,479	Mersin	3,534,082	Mersin	3,688,574	Algeciras (Spain)	4,302,783	Gioia Tauro	5,257,012
Izmir	2,012,460	Algeciras (Spain)	2,433,355	Marsaxlokk (Malta)	2,557,909	Mersin	2,922,011	Algeciras (Spain)	3,314,085	Algeciras (Spain)	3,481,666	Leghorn	4,095,705	Tanger Med (Morocco)	4,563,962
Mersin	2,000,481	Leghorn	2,409,924	Mersin	2,505,192	Leghorn	2,691,614	Tanger Med (Morocco)	3,169,339	Tanger Med (Morocco)	3,364,336	Tanger Med (Morocco)	4,015,977	Leghorn	4,001,102
Beirut	1,967,722	Mersin	2,252,146	Alexandria	2,501,881	Haifa	2,478,705	Evyap	2,795,377	Evyap	2,976,050	Mersin	3,925,325	Evyap	3,764,568
Piraeus	1,937,204	Alexandria	2,226,517	Beirut	2,335,620	Leghorn	2,472,355	Gemlik	2,630,104	Gemlik	2,861,707	Evyap	3,799,404	Mersin	3,568,112
Algeciras (Spain)	1,828,384	Haifa	2,136,984	Haifa	2,315,626	Tanger Med (Morocco)	2,386,676	Leghorn	2,586,829	Leghorn	2,806,108	Haifa	3,048,306	Haifa	3,309,228
Haifa	1,645,654	Beirut	2,066,708	Naples	2,292,448	Beirut	2,308,888	Beirut	2,391,259	Beirut	2,658,565	Gemlik	2,886,688	Ashdod	3,021,836
Ashdod	1,604,847	Ashdod	1,966,588	Ashdod	2,228,308	Evyap	2,298,841	Ashdod	2,334,412	Ashdod	2,592,411	Ashdod	2,800,649	Beirut	2,875,766
Alexandria	1,410,562	Izmir	1,617,251	Tanger Med (Morocco)	2,213,778	Izmir	2,206,155	Haifa	2,251,110	Haifa	2,476,325	Nemrut Bay	2,659,821	Gemlik	2,871,164
Limassol	1,365,696	Limassol	1,412,537	Izmir	2,016,813	Ashdod	2,042,897	El Dekheila	2,176,434	El Dekheila	2,452,322	Beirut	2,584,637	Nemrut Bay	2,700,588
El Dekheila	1,214,434	Koper (Slovenia)	1,394,327	Gemlik	1,957,398	Trieste (Italy)	2,031,453	Izmir	1,940,675	Izmir	2,395,988	Koper (Slovenia)	2,477,560	Sines (Portugal)	2,570,640

Source: World Bank calculations based on data from Lloyd's List Intelligence.
a. Data cover only May and June.

TABLE 2C.2 **Betweenness centrality, 2009–16** (number of occurrences of port nodes on shortest path)

PORT	2009	PORT	2010	PORT	2011	PORT	2012	PORT	2013	PORT	2014	PORT	2015	PORT	2016[a]
Barcelona	1,481	Alexandria	1,717	Ambarli (Turkey)	2,088	Ambarli (Turkey)	2,158	Valencia (Spain)	1,943	Alexandria	2,278	Alexandria	2,997	Marsaxlokk (Malta)	2,210
Gioia Tauro	1,279	Gioia Tauro	1,476	Marsaxlokk (Malta)	1,931	Valencia (Spain)	1,837	Marsaxlokk (Malta)	1,932	Ambarli (Turkey)	2,276	Alexandria	2,567	Alexandria	1,809
Valencia (Spain)	1,168	Ambarli (Turkey)	1,342	Nemrut Bay	1,692	Algeciras (Spain)	1,489	Ravenna	1,816	Algeciras (Spain)	2,147	Piraeus	2,120	Piraeus	1,464
Izmir	1,093	Marsaxlokk (Malta)	1,152	Ravenna	1,510	Marsaxlokk (Malta)	1,197	Piraeus	1,672	Marsaxlokk (Malta)	2,034	Algeciras (Spain)	2,023	Algeciras (Spain)	1,396
Constantza	1,078	Barcelona	1,070	Gioia Tauro	1,479	Alexandria	1,197	Algeciras (Spain)	1,664	Valencia (Spain)	1,940	Gioia Tauro	1,769	Gioia Tauro	1,167
Iraklion	1,071	Piraeus	1,013	Nemrut Bay	1,360	Nemrut Bay	1,046	Ambarli (Turkey)	1,622	Piraeus	1,563	Ambarli (Turkey)	1,650	Ambarli (Turkey)	1,110
Ceuta	974	Tartous	985	Constantza	1,304	Gioia Tauro	1,027	Alexandria	1,307	Gioia Tauro	1,490	Barcelona	1,482	Barcelona	1,000
Ambarli (Turkey)	959	Nemrut Bay	961	Mersin	1,212	Algeciras (Spain)	962	Ortona	1,060	Nemrut Bay	1,328	Valencia (Spain)	1,448	Valencia (Spain)	990
Marsaxlokk (Malta)	958	Ceuta	934	Alexandria	1,199	Diliskelesi	876	Barcelona	944	Iskenderun	1,316	Iskenderun	1,000	Iskenderun	667
Mersin	832	Mersin	921	Venice	1,140	Izmir	874	Nemrut Bay	830	Odessa	1,221	Izmir	938	Izmir	661
Alexandria	811	Genoa	882	Constantza	1,128	Casablanca	840	Genoa	771	Barcelona	1,045	Cagliari	900	Cagliari	641
Gemlik	736	Taranto	859	Misurata	1,127	Gemlik	784	Beirut	764	Ashdod	953	Thessaloniki	845	Thessaloniki	638
Genoa	730	Valencia (Spain)	815	Izmir	1,061	Misurata	775	Diliskelesi	731	Casablanca	933	Haifa	844	Haifa	638
Limassol	690	Fos	803	Beirut	930	Algiers	749	Izmir	728	Damietta (Egypt, Arab Rep.)	906	Nemrut Bay	803	Nemrut Bay	575
Piraeus	598	Alicante	795	Casablanca	901	Genoa	697	Gioia Tauro	706	Haifa	893	Genoa	791	Genoa	543
Cagliari	577	Constantza	792	Yenikoy	810	Barcelona	672	Tuzla	688	Mersin	841	Ashdod	700	Ashdod	537
Tartous	534	Izmir	771	Haifa	772	Mersin	604	Sulina	650	Tanger Med (Morocco)	679	Fos	652	Fos	483
Algeciras (Spain)	529	La Spezia	749	Mersin	747	Antalya	563	Mersin	626	Salerno	666	El Dekheila	609	El Dekheila	448
Thessaloniki	517	Benghazi	749	Tanger Med (Morocco)	728	La Spezia	562	Gemlik	536	Annaba	654	Trieste (Italy)	574	Trieste (Italy)	446
Tarragona	502	Izmit	659	Salerno	727	Ravenna	531	Damietta (Egypt, Arab Rep.)	524	Algiers	653	Algiers	561	Algiers	372

Source: World Bank calculations based on data from Lloyd's List Intelligence.
a. Data cover only May and June.

TABLE 2C.3 **Degree centrality, 2009–16 (number of links to topologically adjacent neighbor nodes)**

PORT	2009	PORT	2010	PORT	2011	PORT	2012	PORT	2013	PORT	2014	PORT	2015	PORT	2016[a]
Gioia Tauro	71	Gioia Tauro	69	Marsaxlokk (Malta)	72	Marsaxlokk (Malta)	71	Marsaxlokk (Malta)	74	Marsaxlokk (Malta)	72	Marsaxlokk (Malta)	74	Marsaxlokk (Malta)	66
Valencia (Spain)	69	Marsaxlokk (Malta)	69	Valencia (Spain)	67	Valencia (Spain)	68	Valencia (Spain)	64	Algeciras (Spain)	68	Algeciras (Spain)	69	Piraeus	59
Barcelona	67	Piraeus	66	Ambarli (Turkey)	67	Ambarli (Turkey)	66	Piraeus	63	Ambarli (Turkey)	68	Ambarli (Turkey)	66	Gioia Tauro	54
Marsaxlokk (Malta)	66	Izmir	64	Piraeus	61	Gioia Tauro	65	Algeciras (Spain)	63	Valencia (Spain)	64	Valencia (Spain)	64	Algeciras (Spain)	53
Izmir	65	Ambarli (Turkey)	64	Valencia (Spain)	61	Piraeus	64	Gioia Tauro	61	Piraeus	60	Piraeus	64	Ambarli (Turkey)	51
Piraeus	63	Valencia (Spain)	62	Algeciras (Spain)	57	Algeciras (Spain)	57	Ambarli (Turkey)	57	Alexandria	59	Alexandria	63	Alexandria	50
Ambarli (Turkey)	62	Barcelona	61	Izmir	56	Alexandria	55	Alexandria	57	Nemrut Bay	56	Gioia Tauro	59	Valencia (Spain)	47
Genoa	58	Alexandria	61	Barcelona	52	Mersin	54	Nemrut Bay	53	Barcelona	56	Nemrut Bay	56	Nemrut Bay	43
Mersin	58	Genoa	58	Nemrut Bay	52	Izmir	52	Barcelona	53	Alexandria	51	Barcelona	50	Izmir	42
Alexandria	57	Mersin	57	Barcelona	51	Nemrut Bay	51	Genoa	52	Genoa	50	Gemlik	45	El Dekheila	41
Cagliari	52	La Spezia	52	Izmir	50	Barcelona	50	Izmir	50	Izmir	48	Tanger Med (Morocco)	45	Barcelona	38
Gemlik	49	Nemrut Bay	52	Gemlik	49	Genoa	48	Mersin	46	Mersin	47	Mersin	43	Mersin	37
La Spezia	49	Cagliari	51	Nemrut Bay	48	Misurata	46	Gemlik	43	Haifa	47	Haifa	43	Haifa	37
Salerno	48	Gemlik	50	Radès	47	Gemlik	45	La Spezia	43	La Spezia	44	La Spezia	42	Genoa	37
Thessaloniki	46	Algeciras (Spain)	49	Cagliari	46	La Spezia	43	Damietta (Egypt, Arab Rep.)	41	Ashdod	43	Ashdod	42	Gemlik	34
Naples	45	Salerno	46	Leghorn	46	Cagliari	43	La Spezia	40	Beirut	42	Beirut	41	Cagliari	34
Lattakia	44	Taranto	45	Naples	45	Tanger Med (Morocco)	43	Ashdod	40	Izmir	42	Izmir	40	Tanger Med (Morocco)	33
Algeciras (Spain)	43	Naples	44	Tanger Med (Morocco)	44	Ashdod	42	Algiers	40	Damietta (Egypt, Arab Rep.)	40	Damietta (Egypt, Arab Rep.)	40	Algiers	32
Ashdod	43	Casablanca	44	Limassol	44	Algiers	41	Cagliari	39	Algiers	39	Algiers	40	La Spezia	31
Casablanca	43	Thessaloniki	43	Beirut	44	Damietta (Egypt, Arab Rep.)	41	Tanger Med (Morocco)	38	Casablanca	39	Casablanca	40	Ashdod	30

Source: World Bank calculations based on data from Lloyd's List Intelligence.
a. Data cover only May and June.

TABLE 2C.4 **Clustering coefficient, 2009–16 (inverse values)**

PORT	2009	PORT	2010	PORT	2011	PORT	2012	PORT	2013	PORT	2014	PORT	2015	PORT	2016a
Syros	15.0	Termini Imerese	6.0	Sulina	5.0	Dortyol	6.0	Sulina	10.0	Sulina	7.5	Gallipoli	10.0	Porto Nogaro	5.3
Bari	6.0	Ceuta	3.2	Gebze	4.4	Marina di Carrara	4.2	Escombreras	3.5	Ortona	7.0	Ortona	6.0	Arzew	4.2
Iskenderun	4.2	Marsa el Brega	3.1	Zeytinburnu	3.5	Marsaxlokk (Malta)	3.5	Monfalcone	3.0	Zante	7.0	Marsaxlokk (Malta)	3.7	Marsaxlokk (Malta)	3.9
Gallipoli	3.3	Derince	3.0	Chioggia	3.3	Valencia (Spain)	3.4	Eleusis	3.0	Ambarli (Turkey)	7.0	Monfalcone	3.5	Monfalcone	3.3
Brindisi	3.0	Galatz	3.0	Constantza	3.3	Chioggia	3.3	Chioggia	3.0	Marsaxlokk (Malta)	6.0	Ambarli (Turkey)	3.3	Brindisi	3.3
Djen	3.0	Nea Moudhania	3.0	Ambarli (Turkey)	3.2	Djen	3.2	Ortona	3.0	Alexandria	6.0	Marsaxlokk (Malta)	3.3	Ambarli (Turkey)	3.3
Gabes	3.0	Yuzhnyy	3.0	Tuzla	3.0	Sibenik	3.0	Dortyol	3.0	Algeciras (Spain)	5.3	Alexandria	3.3	Algeciras (Spain)	3.2
Termini Imerese	3.0	Ambarli (Turkey)	2.9	Monfalcone	3.0	Ceuta	3.0	Valencia (Spain)	3.0	Porto Nogaro	3.5	Algeciras (Spain)	3.2	Gioia Tauro	3.2
Ceuta	2.9	Gioia Tauro	2.9	Marsaxlokk (Malta)	3.0	Ambarli (Turkey)	3.0	Marsaxlokk (Malta)	2.9	Valencia (Spain)	3.1	Porto Nogaro	3.2	Piraeus	3.1
Barcelona	2.8	Marina di Carrara	2.9	Gioia Tauro	2.9	Nemrut Bay	3.0	Piraeus	2.9	Augusta	3.0	Valencia (Spain)	3.1	Casablanca	3.1
Valencia (Spain)	2.8	Tartous	2.9	Tartous	2.8	Algeciras (Spain)	2.9	Motril	2.9	Monfalcone	3.0	Augusta	3.0	Chioggia	3.0
Izmir	2.7	Nemrut Bay	2.8	Nemrut Bay	2.7	Gebze	2.8	Gallipoli	2.8	Dortyol	3.0	Monfalcone	3.0	Gebze	3.0
Gioia Tauro	2.7	Marsaxlokk (Malta)	2.7	Piraeus	2.7	Piraeus	2.7	Tobruk	2.7	Zelenika	3.0	Dortyol	3.0	Alexandria	3.0
Marsaxlokk (Malta)	2.6	Piraeus	2.7	Marsaxlokk (Malta)	2.8	Gioia Tauro	2.7	Lesport	2.7	Nador	3.0	Nador	3.0	Valencia (Spain)	2.9
Ambarli (Turkey)	2.6	Valletta	2.6	Nemrut Bay	2.7	Sousse	2.7	Perama	2.6	Sete	3.0	Sete	3.0	Barcelona	2.7
Constantza	2.6	Alexandria	2.6	Ceuta	2.6	Alexandria	2.5	Zarzis	2.5	Tenes	3.0	Tenes	3.0	Izmir	2.6
Iraklion	2.5	Barcelona	2.6	Casablanca	2.6	Huelva	2.5	Tuzla	2.5	Piraeus	2.9	Piraeus	2.9	Durres	2.5
Marina di Carrara	2.5	Izmir	2.6	Gemlik	2.5	Bejaia	2.5	Ceuta	2.5	Casablanca	2.9	Casablanca	2.9	Genoa	2.5
Yarimca	2.5	Taranto	2.6	Marina di Carrara	2.6	Tanger Med (Morocco)	2.5	Pozzallo	2.5	Algeciras (Spain)	2.9	Barcelona	2.9	Nemrut Bay	2.4
Genoa	2.5	Augusta	2.5	Eleusis	2.5	Sfax	2.5	Evyap	2.4	Ambarli (Turkey)	2.9	Gioia Tauro	2.9	Haifa	2.4

Source: World Bank calculations based on data from Lloyd's List Intelligence.
a. Data cover only May and June.

NOTES

1. The Herfindahl-Hirschmann index corresponds to the square of the market shares (generally, multiplied by 100) of all the elements of a given sector.
2. The Gamma index is the number of actual links as a percentage of the total possible number of links in a network. It is also referred to as "network density." (Ducruet and Beauguitte 2014).
3. To allow for a longer period of comparison (2009–16), the traffic figures for 2016 were doubled.
4. See http://trajpop.parisgeo.cnrs.fr for details.
5. Single linkage analysis retains each port node's largest flow link with another port and removes all the other links. It has the advantage of revealing the main hubs of the network as well as barrier effects on the shipping network (Nystuen and Dacey 1961).
6. Following Ducruet Itoh, and Merk (2014), extreme values over 30 days were excluded to reduce the noise in the results.
7. The 10 indicators were total twenty-foot equivalent unit traffic (log value), degree of centrality (number of links to adjacently connected ports), betweenness centrality (number of occurrences of ports on shortest paths), proximity to the network's topological center (eccentricity), share of the largest flow link in total twenty-foot equivalent unit traffic (inverse), share of extra-Mediterranean traffic in total twenty-foot equivalent unit traffic, hub power of the node (inverse of the clustering coefficient), average ship turnaround time (number of days), share of alliances traffic in total twenty-foot equivalent unit traffic, and distance to the optimal trunk line (kilometers; log value). The basic principle of the analysis is to reveal hidden information on how ports and variables are grouped or opposed along the most statistically significant principal components.
8. On the basis of data in UNCTAD (2016), Lloyd's List Intelligence's data cover nearly 100 percent of the total capacity of the world container fleet for 2015.

REFERENCES

Comtois, C., and J. J. Wang. 2003. "Géopolitique et transports: Nouvelles Perspectives stratégiques dans le détroit de Taiwan." *Etudes Stratégiques* 34 (2): 213–27.

Ducruet, C. 2008. "Hub Dependence in Constrained Economies: The Case of North Korea." *Maritime Policy and Management* 35 (4): 374–88.

———. 2015. *Maritime Networks: Spatial Structures and Time Dynamics*. Routledge Studies in Transport Analysis. London: Routledge.

———. 2017. "Multilayer Dynamics of Complex Spatial Networks: The Case of Global Maritime Flows (1977–2008)." *Journal of Transport Geography* 60: 47–58.

Ducruet, C., and L. Beauguitte. 2014. "Network Science and Spatial Science: Review and Outcomes of a Complex Relationship." *Networks and Spatial Economics* 14 (3–4): 297–316.

Ducruet, C., H. Itoh, and O. Merk. 2014. "Time Efficiency at World Container Ports." International Transport Forum Discussion Paper 2014–08. Paris: Organisation for Co-operation and Development. http://www.oecd-ilibrary.org/transport/time-efficiency-at-world-container-ports_5jrw2z46t56l-en.

Ducruet, C., and T. E. Notteboom. 2012. "The Worldwide Maritime Network of Container Shipping: Spatial Structure and Regional Dynamics." *Global Networks* 12 (3): 395–423.

Frémont, A. 2007. "Global Maritime Networks: The Case of Maersk." *Journal of Transport Geography* 15 (6): 431–42.

———. 2015. "A Geo-History of Maritime Networks since 1945: The Case of the Compagnie Générale Transatlantique's Transformation into CMA-CGM." In *Maritime Networks: Spatial Structures and Time Dynamics*, edited by C. Ducruet. Routledge Studies in Transport Analysis. London: Routledge: 37–49.

Hu, Y., and D. Zhu. 2009. "Empirical Analysis of the Worldwide Maritime Transportation Network." *Physica A* 388 (10): 2061–71.

Lau, Y. Y., C. Ducruet, A. K. Y. Ng, and X. Fu. 2017. "Across the Waves: A Bibliometric Analysis of Container Shipping Research since the 1960s." *Maritime Policy and Management* 44 (6): 667–84.

McCalla, R. J., B. Slack, and C. Comtois. 2004. "The Geographical Hierarchy of Container Shipping Networks in the Caribbean Basin and Mediterranean Sea." Paper presented at the 10th World Conference on Transport Research, Istanbul, July 4–8.

Nystuen, J. D., and M. F. Dacey. 1961. "A Graph Theory Interpretation of Nodal Regions." *Papers in Regional Science* 7 (1): 29–42.

Rimmer, P. J., and C. Comtois. 2005. "China's Extra- and Intra-Asian Liner Shipping Connections, 1990–2000." *Journal of International Logistics and Trade* 3: 75–97.

UNCTAD (United Nations Conference on Trade and Development). 2017. *Review of Maritime Transport 2017*. United Nations. Geneva.

Zohil, J., and M. Prijon. 1999. "The MED Rule: The Interdependence of Container Throughput and Transshipment Volumes in the Mediterranean Ports." *Maritime Policy and Management* 26 (2): 175–93.

3 Hinterland Connectivity

This chapter analyzes five indicators of hinterland connectivity and presents five case studies of ports that show what has and has not worked in improving hinterland connectivity.

The hinterland of a port can be broadly defined as the region that uses the port to send goods to or receive goods from overseas ports. The hinterland of a port is served by road, rail, and inland waterways (barges). The foreland of a port consists of the overseas destinations served.[1] Working out a hinterland's size is a thorny issue (box 3.1).

INDICATORS OF HINTERLAND CONNECTIVITY

Indicators of hinterland connectivity can best be approached by selecting on a case by case basis from a menu of five indicators (table 3.1). Because data availability is often limited, it can be pragmatic to select only two or three indicators.

Hinterland volume

The first and most basic indicator is the volume of containers to and from the hinterland. Ports generally publish their total volume but rarely break it down into hinterland and transshipment volumes. The conventional definition of total volume comprises empty containers to and from the hinterland, short-sea shipping containers, and containers unloaded in the port that are stored or modified in warehouses in the port and subsequently re-exported overseas.

Of the largest ports in the Mediterranean (and some secondary ports with substantial volumes), Valencia (Spain) and Marseilles have large hinterland volume (table 3.2). (See the next section for a case study of Marseilles.)

BOX 3.1

The size of a port's hinterland

An elementary but theoretically complex question deals with the size of a port's hinterland. Because the hinterland consists of all areas where a port has competitive generalized transport costs (out of pocket costs for transport as well as additional costs, of which inventory costs are generally the most important) relative to competing ports, it can be assessed only against other ports. There are no clear boundaries between hinterlands; some ports have market shares in contestable hinterlands (a hinterland where ports compete for cargo, in contrast to a captive hinterland, where one port has a substantial cost advantage over competing ports; the boundary between is, of course, blurred), and hinterlands differ by cargo type, type of actor, and overseas destination. Nor are hinterlands stable over time. Thus any effort to precisely delimit the hinterland of a port is conceptually flawed.

In addition, any method of identifying the hinterland of a port at a certain moment in time is of limited value because the identified hinterland may not remain the most efficient way to serve port users. These issues—and an approach that shows the regions where a port either has significant market share or can aspire to it—are discussed in annex 3A.

TABLE 3.1 **Indicators of hinterland connectivity**

INDICATOR	DATA AVAILABILITY
Hinterland volume	Often publicly available from either port authority or national statistical agency
Modal split	Limited, rarely publicly available, though some port authorities (for example, Rotterdam and Barcelona) and national statistical agencies (for example, Spain's National Statistics Institute) report it
Intermodal connectivity	Requires substantial data collection effort, generally through contact with rail operators and the port authority at each port
Road congestion	Secondary data collection sourced from publicly available data is generally feasible
Corridor governance	Secondary data collection sourced from publicly available data is generally feasible; definitional issues need to be addressed

Source: Based on port performance measurement by PORTOPIA.
Note: This menu is for containers, which carry the largest share of trade by value and which generally face most of the challenges of efficient access to the hinterland (because most bulk users either are in the port or have invested in dedicated transport systems to transport cargo to their sites in the hinterland).

TABLE 3.2 **Hinterland volume of selected Mediterranean ports, 2015**

PORT	COUNTRY	HINTERLAND VOLUME (TWENTY-FOOT EQUIVALENT UNITS)
Alexandria	Egypt, Arab Rep.	735,000
Algeciras	Spain	380,000
Algiers	Algeria	850,000
Ambarli	Turkey	—
Benghazi	Libya	150,000
Casablanca	Morocco	—
Genoa	Italy	—
Gioia Tauro	Italy	180,000
Marseilles	France	1,200,000
Mersin	Turkey	—
Piraeus	Greece	600,000

(continued)

TABLE 3.2, Continued

PORT	COUNTRY	HINTERLAND VOLUME (TWENTY-FOOT EQUIVALENT UNITS)
Radès	Tunisia	—
Sines	Portugal	260,000
Tanger Med	Morocco	—
Valencia	Spain	2,200,000

Source: Port authority websites.
Note: Marsaxlokk (Malta) and Port Said (the Arab Republic of Egypt) are not included because they hardly serve their hinterlands at all; — = not available.

TABLE 3.3 **Modal split of selected Mediterranean ports, 2015**

PORT	COUNTRY	SHARE OF TOTAL GATEWAY CARGO TRANSPORTED BY RAIL OR BARGE (PERCENT)
Alexandria	Egypt, Arab Rep.	—
Algeciras	Spain	Around 2
Algiers	Algeria	0
Ambarli	Turkey	n.a. (probably 0)
Benghazi	Libya	0
Casablanca	Morocco	—
Genoa	Italy	—
Gioia Tauro	Italy	—
Marseilles	France	17
Mersin	Turkey	—
Piraeus	Greece	Less than 1
Radès	Tunisia	—
Sines	Portugal	—
Tanger Med	Morocco	—
Valencia	Spain	5

Source: Port authority websites.
Note: Marsaxlokk (Malta) and Port Said (Egypt) are not included because they hardly serve their hinterlands at all; — = not available.

Modal split

An increasingly widely used indicator, especially for containers, modal split shows the share of total hinterland container volume[2] to and from the port transported by rail or barge. The calculation method is rail or barge volume divided by total gateway cargo (that is, total container volume minus transshipment volume).

For most countries, calculating this indicator requires data from the container terminal, which measures the hinterland volume, and data from rail terminals in the port, which measure the volume by train. For some countries statistical agencies derive modal split statistics from transport manifests or customs declarations.

Of the largest ports in the Mediterranean (and some secondary ports with substantial volumes), Marseilles has the highest share of rail and barge in the modal split (table 3.3).

Intermodal connectivity

Intermodal connectivity can be calculated when container train and barge[3] schedules are publicly available, which is increasingly the case because publicly providing schedule information is part of the marketing efforts of train and barge operators to attract individual shippers. This type of data is often available on platforms that have schedule information from multiple service providers (for example, www.intermodallinks.com for Europe). With such data, several methods can be used to express a port's connectivity. The simplest indicator is the sum of the unique directly served destinations from a port. More complicated indicators attribute a link quality to each link and then sum the link qualities of all unique destinations. Components[4] of link quality (between port A and inland terminal B) are (De Langen et al. 2017):

- Frequency of the link (higher frequency leads to higher link quality).
- Capacity of the services (greater capacity leads to higher link quality).
- Number of competing service providers (more providers lead to higher link quality).
- Minimum number of intermediate stops (more intermediate stops lead to lower link quality).
- Transit time (longer transit time leads to lower link quality).

Comparing hinterland connectivity across ports is not as useful as comparing maritime connectivity across ports because ports serve different hinterlands. For example, London Gateway predominantly serves one metropolitan area within 100 kilometers and thus hardly relies on intermodal connectivity, while Gioia Tauro serves population centers more than 1,000 kilometers away. The evolution over time of hinterland connectivity can be usefully measured and compared.[5]

Of the largest ports in the Mediterranean (and some secondary ports with substantial volumes), Marseilles is the only one with many unique, inland intermodal destinations on national territory—21—via rail or barge (table 3.4). It is followed by Valencia, Spain (5), and Sines, Portugal (3). And only Marseilles

TABLE 3.4 **Intermodal connectivity of selected Mediterranean ports, 2016**

PORT	COUNTRY	UNIQUE INTERMODAL DESTINATIONS	CONNECTIONS OUTSIDE HOME COUNTRY?	DESTINATIONS
Alexandria	Egypt, Arab Rep.	—	No	
Algeciras	Spain	1	No	Madrid
Algiers	Algeria	0	No	
Ambarli	Turkey	— (probably 0)	No	
Benghazi	Libya	0	No	
Casablanca	Morocco	—	No	
Genoa	Italy	—	Yes	
Gioia Tauro	Italy	1	No	Nola

(continued)

TABLE 3.4, *Continued*

PORT	COUNTRY	UNIQUE INTERMODAL DESTINATIONS	CONNECTIONS OUTSIDE HOME COUNTRY?	DESTINATIONS
Marseilles	France	21	Yes	Valence, Mâcon, Lyon, Toulouse, Châlon-sur-Saône, Dijon, Bordeaux, Cognac, Strasbourg, Paris, Le Havre, Dourges, Dunkirk, Munich, Ludwigshafen, Duisburg, Hamburg, Lübeck, Rotterdam, Antwerp, Zeebrugge[a]
Mersin	Turkey	—	Probably not	—
Piraeus	Greece	1	No	Thessaloniki
Radès	Tunisia	—	Probably not	—
Sines	Portugal	3	No	Entrocamento, Lisbon, Setúbal
Tanger Med	Morocco	—	No	—
Valencia	Spain	5	No	Bilbao, Madrid, San Roque, Seville, Vigo

Source: Intermodal Links website (www.intermodallinks.com) and port authority websites.
Note: Marsaxlokk (Malta) and Port Said (Egypt) are not included because they hardly serve their hinterlands at all; — = not available.
a. French inland ports are listed first, followed by German, Dutch and Belgian inland ports.

definitely serves inland nodes in a third country: Germany (5), Belgium (2), and the Netherlands (1).

Road congestion

Even though intermodal transport is becoming more important, in virtually all ports the vast majority of landside moves are by truck, so an indicator on road congestion is useful. Congestion can occur on port access roads and in truck queues for terminals. Only a few ports provide publicly available information on truck waiting and turnaround times. The port of Vancouver publishes waiting times online,[6] the port of Montreal has an app with truck waiting times,[7] the port of Oakland has sensors along the streets leading up to its terminals to track how long truck drivers wait to pick up cargo, APM Terminals publicly reports truck waiting times at its terminal in Gothenburg, and the ports of Los Angeles and Long Beach measure truck waiting times but do not make the data public. These initiatives are a part of a broader approach to improve landside efficiency, where the port authority, terminals, and public institutions cooperate.

New technology using information from phones and other devices in cars to provide real-time data on congestion is becoming more widespread. The company with the most publicly available data is Waze (www.waze.com), which provides data on current and historical road congestion. The Waze data are especially useful when monitored over time.

Figure 3.1 presents data on road congestion near Algeciras (Spain) and Piraeus. There is no road congestion to and from Algeciras (Spain), but for Piraeus there is some congestion in the morning and a very small congestion peak in the late afternoon, in line with rush-hour patterns. In absolute terms congestion on the access highway to Piraeus is light, with travel taking about 20 minutes longer in the morning than at other times—and generally less than time than handling at the terminal gate (which is reported to be 15–30 minutes).

FIGURE 3.1

Travel time on the main port access road, Algeciras (Spain) and Piraeus, 2016

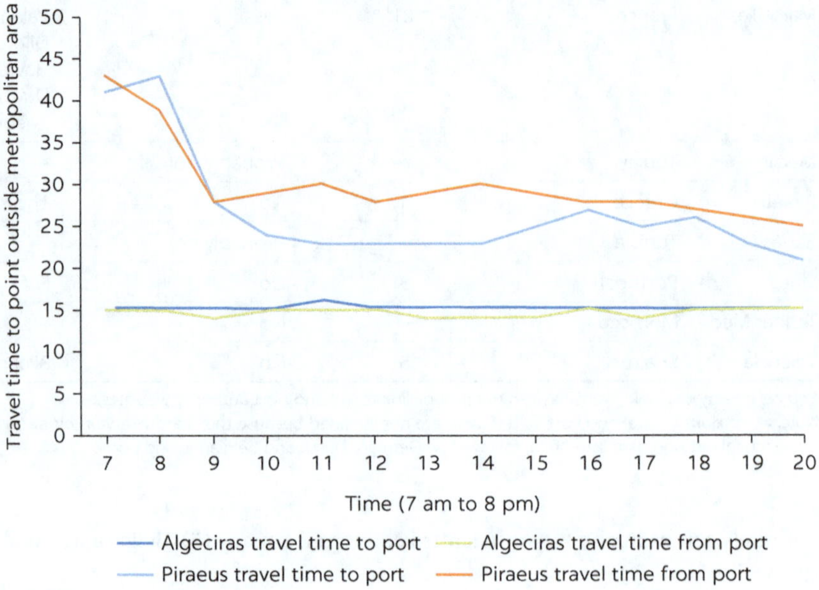

[Chart: Travel time to point outside metropolitan area (y-axis, 0-50) vs. Time 7 am to 8 pm (x-axis, 7-20). Four series: Algeciras travel time to port, Algeciras travel time from port, Piraeus travel time to port, Piraeus travel time from port.]

Source: Based on Waze data.

Corridor governance

The presence of a corridor governance structure along international corridors from a port to the hinterland is another relevant indicator. Hartman (2013) and Kunaka and Carruthers (2014) underline corridor governance as well as performance monitoring along corridors.

In the European Union the concept of core corridors to connect all EU countries is a cornerstone of the EU transport policy. Such EU core corridors have been identified, and an analysis of missing links or bottlenecks has been made for each. The policy aim is to have complete and well-functioning corridors by removing bottlenecks, building missing cross-border connections, and promoting modal integration and interoperability. The EU policy history with trans-European networks started in 1995; in 2013 the current focus on nine EU core corridors was established.

This policy approach has led to corridor governance structures in which a work plan is drawn up for each corridor. To make sure that the corridors are developed effectively and efficiently, each is led by a European coordinator, supported by a consultative forum (the Corridor Forum). The European coordinators periodically deliver a common progress report. North African ports generally do not have corridor governance structures in place.

Five case studies of ports and their hinterlands

This section presents five case studies of ports and their hinterlands. The ports were chosen because they shed light on the challenges regarding improving hinterland access to and from ports.

Barcelona: Developing the hinterland network pays off

Among Mediterranean ports, Barcelona has one of the most active strategies to develop a network of inland ports.[8] It is Spain's third-largest container port, after Valencia and Algeciras. Barcelona is well located to serve other parts of Spain as well as the South of France. However, the port community and the port authority have traditionally focused on Catalonia, a region that has 7.3 million inhabitants (16 percent of the Spanish population) and generates around 19 percent of Spanish GDP.

Truck transport has always been the dominant hinterland transport mode, but the port also has rail sidings at the container terminals and a public rail terminal. Barcelona is connected to four rail corridors: to Madrid, northern Spain, Toulouse (France), and Lyon (France)—and from Lyon to other destinations in central Europe (map 3.1).

In 2003 the Barcelona Port Authority launched a strategic plan for the hinterland; the plan has been expanded over the years. The main goal was to develop the port–hinterland network. In line with the plan the port authority invested in a container depot, logistics zone, and rail terminal, and it extended rail links. It also invested in the rail terminal in Zaragoza in a new intermodal terminal close to Figueras and in the logistics zone in Perpignan (France). These investments provided a base to develop logistics services to attract sea-based cargo.

Zaragoza was the port authority's main early location outside Barcelona and has become a central node in the network.[9] In 2000 the port authority, with other bodies, began with a small investment in a container depot—Terminal Marítima de Zaragoza—next to an existing logistics zone (MercaZaragoza).

MAP 3.1

Barcelona's hinterland network, 2010

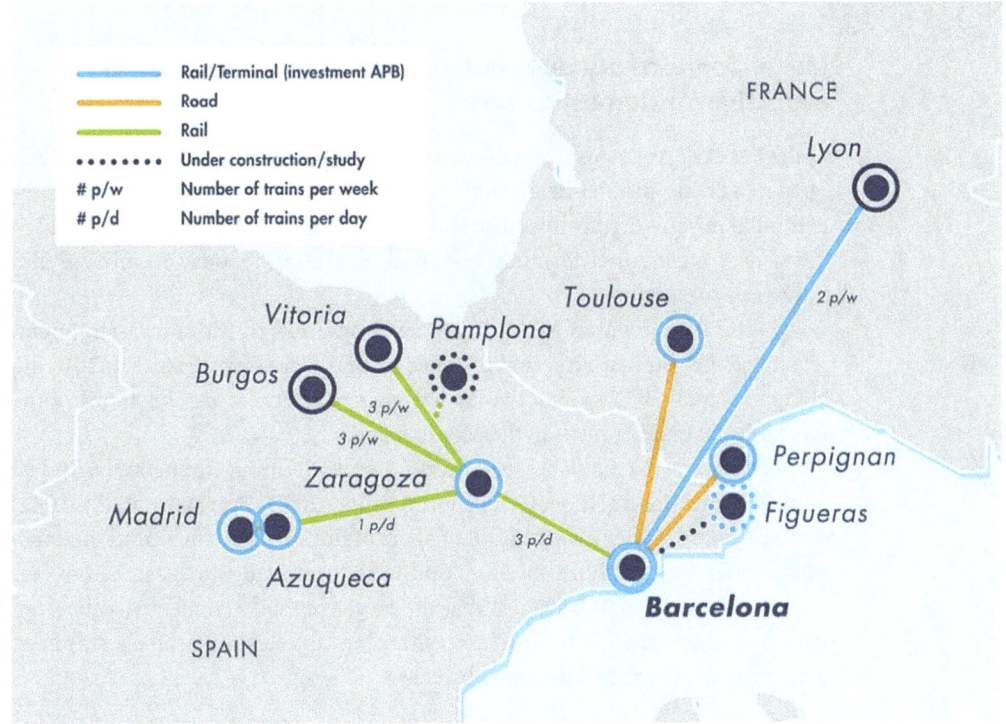

Source: Van den Berg and De Langen 2011 based on data from the Barcelona Port Authority.

TABLE 3.5 **Container traffic statistics for Barcelona (twenty-foot equivalent units, unless otherwise indicated)**

ITEM	2007	2008	2009	2010	2011	2014	2015	2016
Total container volume (thousands)	2,610	2,569	1,800	1,946	2,034	1,893	1,954	2,237
Transshipment volume (thousands)	989	959	606	634	667	312	274	432
Gateway volume, excluding transshipment (percent)	1,621	1,610	1,194	1,313	1,367	1,580	1,680	1,805
Total rail transport (thousands)	42	53	60	104	147	190	213	226
Share of rail transport in total hinterland volume (percent)	2.6	3.3	5.0	7.9	10.7	12.0	12.7	12.5

Source: Van den Berg and De Langen 2011 and data from the Barcelona Port Authority.

In 2006 the port authority increased its involvement and developed a new rail terminal at the terminal with MercaZaragoza and the regional government.

The port authority invested in rail to improve links to the port of Barcelona in order to compete with other ports. Operators were not taking the initiative because of risks, capacity constraints, and lack of management time. In 2009 it joined with Renfe (a Spanish rail operator) and Naviland (a French one) to invest in a rail link to Lyon, 300 kilometers away and outside Barcelona's traditional hinterland.

The hinterland activities have resulted in a modal shift from road to rail (table 3.5). With more than 70,000 twenty-foot equivalent units, the rail terminal in Zaragoza handles the largest volume of the inland terminals.

The data suggest that the port authority's rail strategy has succeeded.[10] The share of rail services has gone up (a modal shift), and market share has been gained in new hinterland markets through promotion and investment in terminals and rail services (a port shift).

Malta: Connectivity does not automatically make shipping attractive for domestic users

Malta lies at a crossroads of north–south and east–west shipping routes. It developed as a center for Mediterranean commerce, and port activities are now concentrated in Valletta (mostly cruise and roll-on, roll-off) and Marsaxlokk (which consists of a container terminal operated by Malta Freeport Terminals[11] and industrial port facilities).

Around 96 percent of Malta Freeport's container traffic is transshipment, given the very limited diversion distance from the east–west route. In 2016 the company handled 3.1 million twenty-foot equivalent units, making it one of the five largest container ports in the Mediterranean.

Malta scores particularly well on the Liner Shipping Connectivity Index. However, the Malta National Transport Strategy 2050 (Transport Malta 2016a) and Transport Master Plan 2025 (Transport Malta 2016b), which cover all transport modes for the short, medium and long term, and European Centre for Strategic Analysis (2017) suggest that the large container connectivity does not translate automatically to attractive shipping services for Maltese shippers. Those reports identify four main obstacles:

- Landside costs are high. This is due partly to landside congestion and partly to the limited competition among trucking service providers

- Port costs for import–export cargo are high. This is because the terminal is fully focused on efficient transshipment operations. The volume of import export cargo is low (around 120,000 twenty-foot equivalent units) and not a priority of the terminal operator. The same also applies to shipping companies, which often aim to call and depart from Malta fully loaded. This creates an upward pressure on rates for import–export
- Reliability is low because the port is sometimes bypassed when there is bad weather or the ship has been delayed in previous ports. This forces shippers to hold large safety stocks
- Imports and exports to Europe could be more cost-effective with roll-on, roll-off, but roll-on, roll-off connectivity is limited and prices are high because of low demand and scant competition.

These points do not suggest that maritime connectivity does not create value but that maritime connectivity does not automatically lead to attractive shipping services for import–export cargo and that a mix of infrastructure investments and regulations may be instrumental in creating value for importers and exporters.

Marseilles: The need for an interterminal rail link

The port of Marseilles has thee container terminals (one close to the city, two in Marseilles Fos, which is around 50 kilometers away) that handled more than 1.2 million twenty-foot equivalent units in 2016 (table 3.6). Marseilles has the largest share of intermodal (rail and barge) transport of all Mediterranean ports: 17 percent in 2016. The port authority (Grand Port Maritime de Marseille) is trying to improve the share of rail and inland waterways in the model split (with some success for rail), in part to improve air quality in the region.

Inland waterway volume declined in 2016, after several years of slight growth. The share of gateway volume by inland waterway was lower in 2016 (6.9 percent) than in 2007 (7.1 percent). Marseilles serves four inland ports in France via inland shipping. These inland ports increasingly cooperate in the organization Medlink, with the aim of improving inland barge volume. The Marseilles Fos port authority chief executive officer currently chairs the Medlink board.

Marseilles serves a substantial number of inland nodes in France and Northern Europe (map 3.2). Most are in the contestable hinterland, where several ports compete for cargo. For instance, just over half the containers arriving at or leaving Lyon pass through the port of Marseilles, even though Marseilles is the closest port to Lyon. The port authority reports transit performance indicators to assess the effectiveness of hinterland services. Some of the destinations served by rail go only through transshipment hubs.

TABLE 3.6 **Inland volume and modal split of Marseilles**

INDICATOR	2014	2015	2016
Total volume (twenty-foot equivalent units)	1,179,910	1,223,071	1,251,744
Gateway volume (twenty-foot equivalent units)	1,146,200	1,178,017	1,205,742
Rail volume (twenty-foot equivalent units)	99,581	112,742	121,595
Share of gateway cargo (percent)	8.7	9.6	10.1
Inland waterway volume (twenty-foot equivalent units)	95,724	99,393	83,254
Share of gateway cargo (percent)	8.4	8.4	6.9

Source: Based on data from the Grand Port Maritime de Marseille.

MAP 3.2
Inland nodes served by Marseilles port, 2016

Source: Based on data from the Grand Port Maritime de Marseille.

The port authority aims to build or expand rail terminals. One project is an interterminal rail link, which would increase the efficiency of rail and bring financial and environmental benefits by reducing road haulage, especially because some train services serve Fos, others Marseilles city.

Port Said East: A newcomer in the already highly competitive market for Egypt's hinterland

Egypt has five container ports within 300 kilometers of each other on its Mediterranean coast. The inevitable result is that none can realize potential efficiencies of scale or number of services to other Mediterranean ports. Their hinterlands largely overlap and are highly competitive.

Port Said East has been operational since 2004 and is the newest of the five ports. With more than 3.5 million twenty-foot equivalent units a year, it has the most container trade. It is at the Mediterranean entrance to the Suez Canal, which is the conduit for 8 percent of the world's maritime trade. It is linked to the canal via a new access channel that can accommodate the largest container ships now afloat.

Port Said East accounts for about 60 percent of Egypt's transshipment containers, and transshipment accounts for 92 percent of the port's total traffic. Competition among the ports' hinterlands is as intense as it is for maritime connectivity. All the Mediterranean ports are within 260 kilometers of each other and within 250 kilometers of the Cairo Metropolitan Area, which has a population of just under 20 million. A hinterland expansion of any one port will intrude on the hinterland of the others.

The hinterlands of Egypt are divided into three groups:

- Alexandria and El Dekheila, with an exclusive hinterland based on the governorate of Alexandria
- Damietta, with a small exclusive hinterland centered on its own governorate
- Port Said East and Port Said West, only about 20 kilometers apart, with an exclusive hinterland that includes the cities and governorates of Port Said and Ismailia and the Mediterranean coast of the Sinai Peninsula, which has an aggregate population of just over 2 million. Its "L" shape extends about 80 kilometers along the Suez Canal and about 200 kilometers along the Mediterranean coast.

While there is little locational advantage for any of the five ports, Port Said East is disadvantaged in not having regular rail services or inland waterway links and in having the highest truck tariffs. It is not the best located for import and export containers, despite being one of the closest ports to the Cairo Metropolitan Area (it is on the other side of the canal).

Access by both road and rail to Port Said East is unreliable. The rail link depends on a swing bridge across the Suez Canal, which until 2015 was closed every time a convoy passed. Now that the convoy system is no longer needed, it can be closed any time a large ship passes. The road bridge was closed for security reasons for almost two years and reopened in 2015. Trucks transporting domestic containers from Port Said East had to be ferried across the canal. The bridge could be closed again at any time for security reasons.

The rail link from Port Said East to the Cairo Metropolitan Area is little used; rail links from the other ports are used a little more. Egyptian railways focus on passenger traffic (500 million passengers a year but only 6 million tons of freight, mostly bulk minerals) and have poor intermodal connections in the Cairo Metropolitan Area. Alexandria/El Dekheila and Damietta have inland waterway connections to the Cairo Metropolitan Area (via canals leading to the Nile River), but they are little used other than for wheat or empty containers. Attempts to expand barge services have met with little success, despite improvements to navigation and the river ports in the Cairo Metropolitan Area. The few domestic containers from Port Said East (around 250,000 twenty-foot equivalent units per year) are trucked to their destination, although the closest Mediterranean port to the Cairo Metropolitan Area has the highest truck tariffs (about $285 for about 185 kilometers).

The hinterland of Port Said East is set to expand (map 3.3). Under the Suez Canal Corridor Development Project the capacity of the canal has been almost doubled and the transit time reduced by about 12 hours. The new 8.5 kilometer long, 18.5 meter deep access channel to Port Said East opened in 2016 and

MAP 3.3
Proposed new facilities to expand the hinterland of East Port Said

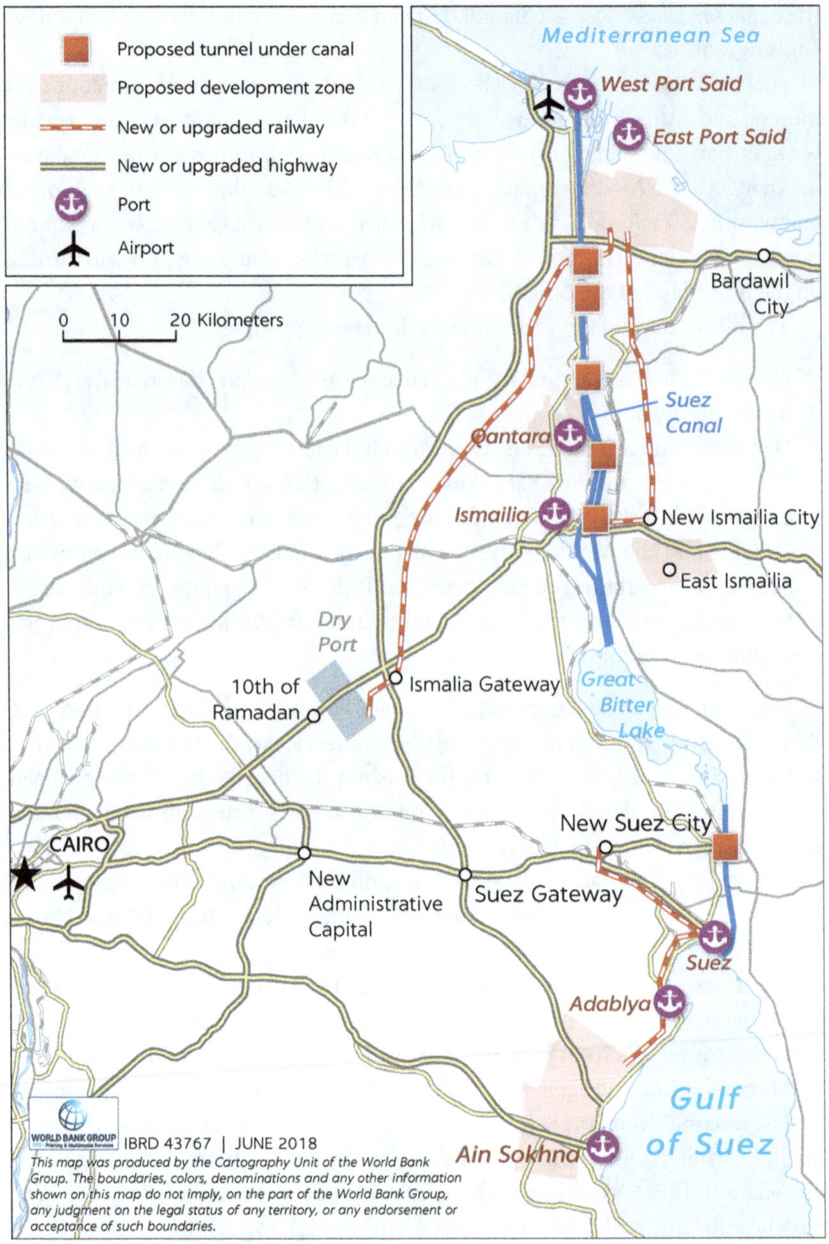

Source: Suez Canal Economic Zone website (https://www.sczone.eg/English/Map/Pages/SCZoneMap.aspx).

guarantees 24/7 access to the port's special economic zone. Port Said East will also get a dedicated rail freight link to a new technology valley being developed at Ismailia and to a dry port at 10th Ramadan, a large suburb of Cairo. A rail tunnel and two new road tunnels will be built under the canal to avoid the port being dependent on bridges over the canal. By improving connectivity, these facilities could make Port Said East the container port with the lowest land access time for more than 25 percent of Egypt's population.

Tanger Med: Capturing gateway cargo requires (time-consuming) infrastructure investments

Tanger Med is two ports in one, located on the Strait of Gibraltar at a crossroads of north–south and east–west maritime routes, which together carry about 20 percent of global trade (map 3.4). However, it is at the northern edge of Morocco, farther than the port of Casablanca from most of the country's population and industry. Since its opening in 2007, it has functioned mainly as a transshipment port (96 percent of its almost 3 million twenty-foot equivalent units are transshipped). It is also a gateway port in competition with Casablanca for most of its hinterland. Tanger Med handles less than 11 percent of Morocco's domestic containers, compared with Casablanca's 74 percent and Agadir's 15 percent.

The transshipment and gateway functions are largely independent of each other. The transshipment business is based on transshipment between deep-sea routes of the main shipping companies as well as hub-and-spoke trade using feeder services mainly to Mediterranean ports. The gateway function is based on proximity to Europe, with roll-on, roll-off and container services to ports in France and Spain, but using the same transshipment feeder services for exports (mostly assembled vehicles) to other African countries and the Middle East.

The Tangier–Tétouan region still accounts for more than 75 percent of the port's domestic trade. The port has become an essential export link for the region's thriving auto components and assembly industry, now the second largest in Africa, and for textiles, clothing, and light manufacturing. The port has excellent road links to the industrial zones of Tangier.

Traffic studies have shown that Tanger Med could capture 30 percent of Morocco's domestic container shipments (almost three times the current share),

MAP 3.4

Tanger Med is two ports in one

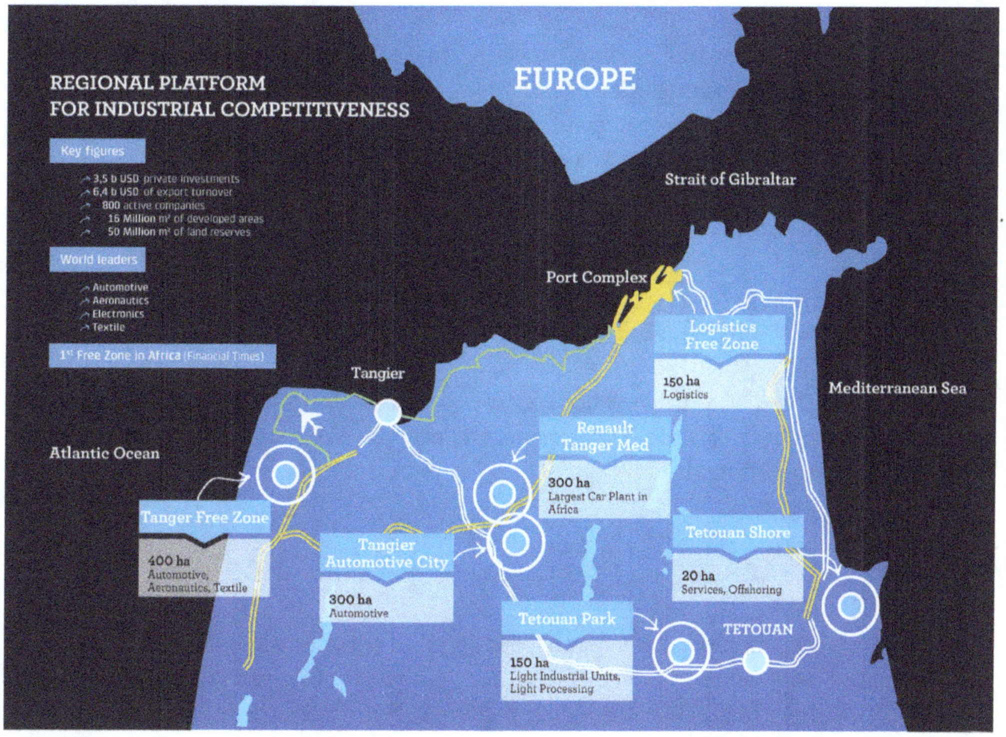

Source: Tanger Med Port Authority.

depending on how much new cargo is generated by investment in industrial production in the greater Tangier area and provided that infrastructure is built to improve access to a large hinterland. (Tanger Med is examined in greater detail in a case study in chapter 4.)

Tanger Med's competitive hinterland with Casablanca includes Fès (Morocco's second-largest city, with about 1.1 million people) and Meknes (about 800,000 people).[12] Fès is about 450 kilometers from Tanger Med but only 290 kilometers from Casablanca; Meknès is 385 kilometers from Tanger Med but only 230 kilometers from Casablanca. The two cities account for only about 16 percent of Morocco's population.

The golden triangle of Kénitra, Meknès, and Tangier is the expected location of much of the growth of Morocco's auto industry, as well as for much of Casablanca's current share of the hinterland, as developers seek to avoid the congestion and high transport and labor costs of the Casablanca urban area. This large area is mostly within the hinterlands of both Casablanca and Tanger Med and will be the focus of hinterland competition between them. The poor connectivity between much of the triangle and Tanger Med will be greatly eased when a new highway connecting Fès, Meknès, and Tangier is completed (construction is scheduled to start in 2018), cutting the travel distance by about 200 kilometers and increasing Tanger Med's role in this growing competitive hinterland.

Tangier has rail access to Casablanca, Marrakech, and Rabat in the south and to Fès, Meknès, and Oujda in the east. Tanger Med is attached to the Moroccan rail network via a container rail terminal with capacity for three roundtrips a day to Casablanca (with a transit time of 12 hours). Tanger Med also has a rail terminal for vehicles that connects the port and Renault's factory in Melloussa (35 kilometers away), as well as a rail terminal for hydrocarbons. A high-speed passenger rail line between Tangier and Casablanca is set to come into operation in 2018, which will free up the existing line and ensure greater rail freight capacity for the port.

Tanger Med accounts for 14 percent of national domestic port traffic (not counting transshipment). Its import–export traffic reached 12.8 million tons in 2016, a 19 percent increase from 2015. The upward trend in domestic traffic in the port is expected to continue over the next few years, given continuing development of industry in the Tangier region, the economic growth of the region, and the expansion of logistics.

ANNEX 3A: IDENTIFYING A PORT'S HINTERLAND

This annex reviews characteristics of port hinterlands, discusses challenges in identifying a port's hinterland, and proposes a basic method for identifying a port's hinterland.

CHARACTERISTICS OF PORT HINTERLANDS

The hinterland of a port depends on the characteristics of the cargo. The most pertinent is the value of time. For instance, for cargo with a low value of time, Rotterdam's hinterland may include Switzerland, because of the low cost but time-consuming barge services running from Rotterdam but not from ports in the Mediterranean. For cargo with a high value of time, Switzerland may be a hinterland for ports further south (for example, Genoa and Venice).

The maritime connectivity of a port heavily influences generalized transport costs and thus the size of a port's hinterland. This connectivity is explained largely by investment in port infrastructure, which can generate scale economies, both in building ports and in port operations (for terminals and shipping companies). Supply chain costs are also lower the larger a port is because better connectivity translates into lower inventory requirements and higher reliability. Because of these scale economies, a small number of ports can handle all container cargo to or from a country or region.[13] For instance, in the United States, a large country, only 32 ports handle more than 50,000 twenty-foot equivalent units per year, and the 10 largest ports handle over 90 percent of total U.S. volume (more than 40 million twenty-foot equivalent units in 2016.

Likewise, intermodal connectivity influences hinterland size. There are scale economies in train and barge hinterland transport. Higher frequencies lead to lower generalized transport costs. These scale economies also foster concentration of intermodal traffic in a few ports. Given the high costs of building and maintaining canals and rail links, such investments are feasible only with high traffic.

A port's hinterland also depends on the competitiveness of direct hinterland transport relative to feedering. For example, port users in the greater Casablanca area can either use Casablanca, in which case most containers will be transshipped (either in Tangier, Morocco, or another transshipment hub), or truck their cargo to Tangier and get a direct service. The balance between feedering and direct trucking also depends on the scale economies through maritime connectivity and intermodal connectivity just discussed.

Institutional aspects, such as tax regimes and border-crossing procedures, influence the size of a port's hinterland, generally favoring domestic over foreign ports.

Behavioral aspects also influence the size of hinterlands. For example, forwarders are more sensitive to out-of-pocket costs while shippers generally are more sensitive to generalized cost components, such as reliability and inventory costs.

Given these characteristics, port hinterlands are path dependent—that is, past patterns affect future development. The main mechanism is first-mover advantage so that ports that have developed certain hinterlands often continue to serve regions with lower generalized transport costs even though from a purely geographic point of view other ports may be better positioned. For instance, Hamburg has a huge market share in Bavaria because of its first-mover advantage, even though from a geographic perspective Koper (Slovenia), Rotterdam, or Trieste (Italy) would seem better positioned for that hinterland.

Challenges in identifying a port's hinterland

Identifying a port's hinterland is problematic for several reasons. The hinterland of a port is relational in that it depends on the overseas origin and destination of the cargo. For instance, the hinterland of the port complex of Los Angeles and Long Beach covers perhaps as much of 60 percent of the continental United States for goods to and from northern East Asia and as little as 20 percent for goods to and from Europe and Africa.

Any method of identifying the hinterland at a certain moment in time is of limited value because the identified hinterland may not remain the most efficient way to serve port users for three reasons:

- Border-crossing costs may be prohibitively expensive and constrain the hinterland of a port, as with parts of Argentina, which could be best served through Chilean ports if border-crossing processes were more efficient
- Ports may be very inefficient or congested or may lack terminal equipment and thus be unable to serve their full hinterland, as with Maputo (Mozambique) and Pecem (Brazil)
- New greenfield port development could change the hinterlands of existing ports.

While the hinterland at a certain moment in time may not be the most efficient, a method to identify an efficient distribution of hinterlands over ports is problematic. Such a method would require an integrated approach rather than an approach focused on minimizing hinterland costs alone. Further, the method would have to deal with the path dependence of port developments (failing to consider investments already made would render the results of little value).[14] Such a method would also be of little use because uncertain future developments (for example, in ship sizes and container volumes) would affect the efficient distribution of the hinterland.

A basic method for identifying a port's hinterland

The method proposed here provides a first indication of the hinterland of a port based on three variables:[15]

- Road distance to the region relative to the road distance from other ports
- Maritime distance to the region relative to the maritime distance from other ports
- Maritime connectivity of the port (function of ship calls and call size) relative to the maritime connectivity of other ports.

Data on these three variables can be used to calculate, for a specific hinterland region, the most optimal port for a certain overseas destination region. The weights of the variables can be based on empirical analysis. The calculation can be treated as a calculation to assess the utility of a certain port for cargo between a certain hinterland region and a certain overseas region:

$$U_{p,h,wr} = \alpha_0^{p,h} + \alpha_1 RD_{p,h} + \alpha_2 MD_{p,wr} + \alpha_3 MC_p$$

where $U_{p,h,wr}$ is the utility of a certain port p for cargo between a certain hinterland region h and a certain overseas region, wr, $RD_{p,h}$ is the road distance between port p and hinterland region h, $MD_{p,wr}$ is the maritime distance between port p and a certain world region, and MC_p is the maritime connectivity of port p. α_1 to α_3 represent the weight of the variables; α_0 can be regarded as an error term.

The most basic model would include these three variables; more variables can be added to this function based on specific considerations. Examples include border crossings, the presence of locks, and the like. The coefficients can be based on estimates in other countries or the country to which the model is applied.

What regions to include

Not all regions may be hinterland regions, and consequently this method may not be relevant. Some regions may be served through feeders instead of the continental modes of truck, train, and barge—for example, remote regions in Canada, Chile, and Norway. For completeness a simple mathematical tool can be used to compare the costs of road hinterland services with the costs of feeder movements between the region and the principal hub. The model does not include the value of time because it is impossible to assess transit time differences between feeders and direct calls. All-road costs are taken to be variable per kilometer (this is generally done in cost models, even though in practice road costs per kilometer are lower for longer trips than for short trips. Thus, a higher rate per kilometer for the last-haul costs in the feeder chain can be used). The feeder costs consist of a variable cost per kilometer for shipping, port costs for handling at the terminal, and variable hinterland costs for the last haul by road.

For the port costs the transshipment rate has to be used. The terminal operating company would charge a direct call combined with road transport to the origin–destination and the import–export fee; the alternative feeder trajectory includes one import–export fee and one transshipment fee. This additional transshipment fee needs to be included when calculating the tradeoff between feedering and hinterland transport. In mathematical terms all road costs, C^{ar}, are expressed as:

$$C^{ar} = VRC^{ar} * ARD \qquad (3A.2)$$

where ARD is the all-road distance (in kilometers) and VRC^{ar} is the variable road costs for the all-road alternative. The feeder costs, C^f, are expressed as:

$$C^f = PC + VRC^f * FRD + VMC * MFD \qquad (3A.3)$$

where PC is the port costs (per twenty-foot equivalent unit), VRC^f is the variable road costs for the feeder alternative, FRD is the last-haul road distance from the feeder port to the final destination, VMC is the variable maritime costs (per kilometer), and MFD is the maritime feeder distance. For any region this formula needs to be calculated for the location least favorable for feedering—that is, with the shortest distance from the deep-sea port and the largest distance from the feeder port (figure 3A.1).[16]

Box 3A.1 provides an example using data for Morocco.

FIGURE 3A.1
The all-road versus feedering costs of a region

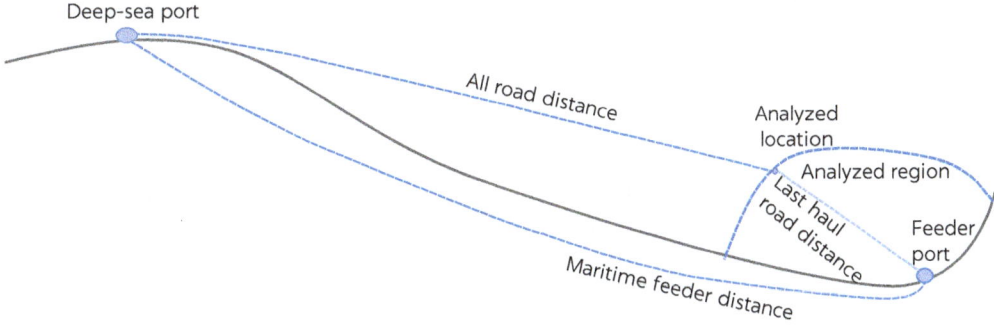

BOX 3A.1

Identifying port hinterlands in Morocco

Four ports are included in the identification of port hinterlands in Morocco: Agadir, Casablanca, Nador, and Tanger Med. Table B3A.1.1 presents a road distance matrix between all regions and these ports. Table B3A.1.2 presents the maritime distance from the four ports to four world regions, as well as the maritime connectivity to them.

These data help identify the hinterland of a port. The analysis includes the three variables mentioned above and a dummy variable for a pure

TABLE B3A.1.1 **Road distance matrix between all regions and the main ports of Morocco (kilometers)**

REGION	AGADIR	CASABLANCA	NADOR	TANGER MED
Agadir	50[a]	467	1,055	836
Al Hoceima	955	552	126	294
Al Jadida	415	102	696	477
Azilal	137	304	744	589
Beni Mellal	450	223	663	508
Boulemane	805	344	389	496
Casablanca	467	50[a]	594	375
Chechaouene	809	332	350	131
El Kelaa des Srarhna	342	207	796	577
Essaouira	220	399	988	769
Fès	750	289	315	441
Figuig	1,376	915	484	1,067
Kaar es Souk	674	534	516	705
Kénitra	597	136	505	248
Khemisset	627	176	429	328
Khenitra	650	264	455	505
Khouribga	466	125	595	495
Marrakech	252	243	832	613
Meknes	721	233	638	385
Nador	1,054	593	50[a]	405
Ouarzazate	329	438	815	808
Oudja	1,070	610	138	761
Rabat	574	87	511	292
Safi	308	236	830	611
Settat	393	77	672	453
Tan Tan	334	775	1,365	1,145
Tanger	794	333	398	53
Taounate	836	375	322	366
Tata	225	659	1,248	1,029
Taza	853	392	248	544
Tétouan	821	360	345	62
Tiznit	98	540	1,129	910

Source: Google Maps.
a. For ports located in the capital city of a province, a distance of 50 kilometers was used.

(continued)

Box 3A.1, *continued*

transshipment port (1 for Tanger Med and 0 for the other three ports).[a] For the weights a_1 to a_3, the coefficients obtained in the empirical analysis of Spain were used (see chapter 4). The utility score of each Moroccan port was calculated for each pair of hinterland regions and world regions, and the hinterland–world region combination was identified as the hinterland of the port with the highest utility score.

Tanger Med's hinterland for trade with the Eastern Mediterranean and Asia covers nearly the entire center of Morocco because of the port's far superior maritime connectivity to these destinations and shorter sailing times (map B3A.1.1). These advantages carry

TABLE B3A.1.2 **Maritime distance and maritime connectivity with four world regions (nautical miles)**

MOROCCAN PORT	EASTERN MEDITERRANEAN AND ASIA	NORTHERN AND CENTRAL EUROPE	NORTH AND CENTRAL AMERICA	WEST AFRICA AND SOUTH AMERICA
Maritime distance				
Agadir	2,346	1,604	4,642	2,258
Casablanca	2,100	1,414	4,770	2,474
Nador	1,804	1,526	4,905	2,790
Tanger Med	1,397	1,370	4,749	2,634
Maritime connectivity[a]				
Agadir	1	12	1	9
Casablanca	1	44	9	19
Nador	0	0	0	0
Tanger Med	100	100	100	100

Source: World Bank's calculations.
a. Normalized so that the port with the highest maritime connectivity has a score of 100.

MAP B3A.1.1

Two hinterlands for Tanger Med, model result, based on 2016 data

a. East Mediterranean and Asia

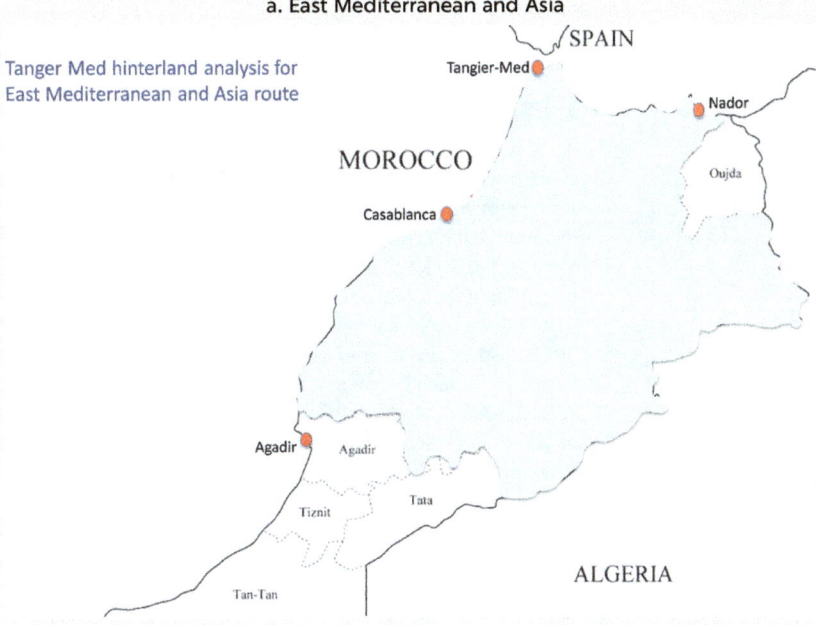

Tanger Med hinterland analysis for East Mediterranean and Asia route

(continued)

Box 3A.1, *continued*

MAP B3A.1.1, *continued*

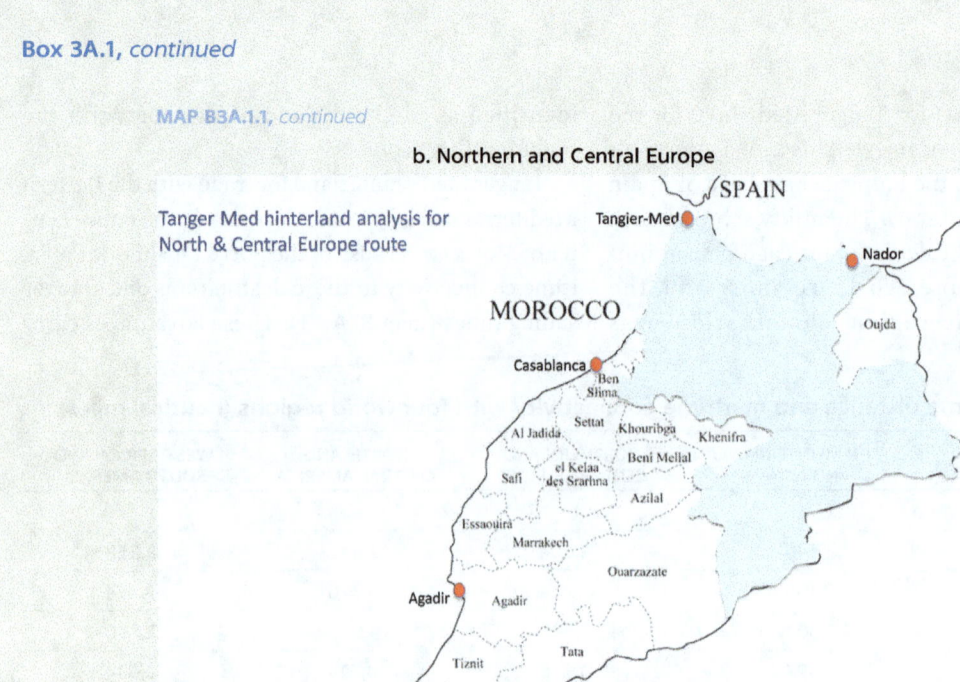

b. Northern and Central Europe

Source: World Bank's calculations.

more weight than the shorter road distances to hinterland regions from Casablanca (and Nador). The hinterland for trade with Northern and Central Europe is limited to northern Morocco because Casablanca has better maritime connectivity with Northern and Central Europe.

a. This dummy variable is included because the analysis of Spain (see chapter 4), as well as the case of Malta, suggests a transshipment focus can hamper the price and quality of the offering for import–export cargo.

NOTES

1. Ports may also serve as intermediate hubs for cargo that arrives and leaves by sea—containers, liquids, and dry bulk. The distinction between hub and gateway traffic is important but blurred in practice. Take the example of Zeebrugge: a container that arrives there and leaves for the United Kingdom on a feeder vessel would be part of the hub function. In contrast, a container that leaves for the United Kingdom by train or ferry, either on a truck or on a trailer, would be part of the gateway function. Notwithstanding these definitional issues, this chapter uses the common definition of the port hinterland as the area to and from which freight moves by truck, train, or inland barge.
2. It is important to express this indicator in relation to hinterland traffic, as the hinterland mode is not relevant for transshipment cargo. Including transshipment traffic in the denominator would mean that the modal split indicator changes with shifts in transshipment traffic. For instance, if Barcelona loses transshipment traffic, its modal split indicator would increase.
3. The remaining analysis focuses on trains because the number of ports with high inland barge traffic is very limited. Of the identified EU core ports, less than 5 percent have container barge services.

4. Some of this information is rarely available.
5. In this case the evolution of the (spatial) economic development of the hinterland may be the most relevant factor in explaining changing intermodal connectivity, in that such changes cannot be attributed to activities and initiatives in ports.
6. See http://www1.portmetrovancouver.com/COGS_Chart/GPSTruck/pmvindex.
7. See http://www.apppicker.com/apps/1147709075/trucking-portal.
8. Other ports active in developing hinterland networks include Rotterdam, Hamburg (where the partially government-owned terminal operator Hamburger Hafen und Logistik AG is heavily involved in developing the rail network), and the port authorities of Los Angeles and Long Beach, which are helping develop the Alameda corridor.
9. The Barcelona Port Authority was previously involved with other ports in two rail terminals around Madrid.
10. Barcelona's rail share is twice that of Valencia and four times that of Algeciras.
11. Malta Freeport Terminals is owned by China Merchants Holdings (through Terminal Link), the shipping line CMA CGM, and Yildirim Group.
12. Morocco's largest metropolitan area is the Casablanca region, with about 5.1 million people. It is about 375 kilometers southwest of Tanger Med and has its own container port. Rabat, with about 1.6 million people, is less than 100 kilometers from Casablanca and 300 kilometers from Tanger Med, so is most likely served from Casablanca when that port has direct connections. The rest of Morocco, further to the south, is served from Casablanca and Agadir.
13. This does not mean that traffic does not shift between ports. This happens frequently, especially for hub ports (for example, Gioia Tauro and Zeebrugge).
14. For example, under such an approach river ports with draft problems, such as Antwerp and Hamburg, would be regarded as inefficient locations for ports. However, given the huge investment in such ports (sunk costs), their continued role in serving their hinterlands is efficient.
15. One could argue that intermodal connectivity should be added. However, in virtually all ports, trucking is the dominant mode—thus a method based purely on road distances may often be good enough.
16. If feedering has lower costs from the location least favorable for feedering, by implication the whole region is best served by feedering. For such a region the analysis of the hinterland from a deep-sea port is not relevant because the region is served predominantly through feedering instead of hinterland transport.

REFERENCES

de Langen, P. W., D. L. Figueroa, K. H. van Donselaar, and J. Bozuwa. 2017. "Intermodal Connectivity in Europe: An Empirical Exploration." *Research in Transportation Business & Management* 23: 3–11.

ECSA (European Centre for Strategic Analysis). 2017. "Mitigating Pressures on the Competitiveness of Manufacturing Activities in Small Peripheral Island States." Research study conducted for the Malta Chamber of Commerce, Enterprise and Industry. Edegem, Belgium.

Hartmann, O. 2013. "Corridor Transport Observatory Guidelines." SSATP Africa Transport Policy Program Working Paper 98. World Bank. Washington, DC. https://openknowledge.worldbank.org/handle/10986/17544.

Kunaka, C., and R. Carruthers. 2014. *Trade and Transport Corridor Management Toolkit*. World Bank. Washington, DC.

Tanger Free Zone. 2015. "TangerMed: Port & Zones." Tangier, Morocco. http://41.77.115.106/~tfz/wp-content/uploads/2015/02/TangerMed_Industrial_Brochure.pdf.

Transport Malta. 2016a. *National Transport Strategy 2050*. Floriana. https://we.tl/KUVohHljLB.

———. 2016b. *Transport Master Plan 2025*. Floriana. https://we.tl/q78hZ6MzcG.

Van den Berg, R., and P. W. De Langen. 2011. "Hinterland Strategies of Port Authorities: A Case Study of the Port of Barcelona." *Research in Transportation Economics* 33 (1): 6–14.

4 Three Case Studies on the Connectivity of Ports

This chapter takes the first steps toward an integrated analysis of how maritime and hinterland connectivity create value for port users and influence the competitiveness of a port. It includes three case studies: a statistical analysis of port market shares in Spain and two studies of maritime and hinterland connectivity of the ports of Port Said (the Arab Republic of Egypt) and Tanger Med (Morocco).

Spain was selected for the statistical analysis because of the publicly available data on the use of ports to and from all Spanish regions.[1] Port Said (Egypt) and Tanger Med (Morocco) were selected because both are primarily transshipment hubs with ambitious initiatives for related economic development, offering possible pointers for other ports.

PORT MARKET SHARES IN SPAIN

While previous studies have provided insights into factors that explain port choice, the relevance of maritime connectivity and hinterland connectivity as explanatory variables for port market share has not been tested empirically. This case study does so using data for Spain and covers 11 ports in 10 regions (table 4.1) and 47 regions (map 4.1), for two years—for a total of 3,760 observations (10 ports * 47 regions in Spain * 4 world regions * 2 years). Annex 4A provides some of the underlying data and explains the methodology for the calculations.

Based on the analysis in the preceding chapters (see, for example figure 1.1 in chapter 1), the (log) likelihood of choosing a port (also known as the market share) depends on three components: port importance and competitive advantage, connectivity between the hinterland and the port, and connectivity between the port and the destination (see annex 4A). Seven variables within these three components were tested for their impact on the market share of a port in a certain hinterland region for trade to a certain world destination:[2]

Port importance and competitive advantage

- Throughput volume of the port (based on the notion of scale economies in port operations, leading to higher productivity and lower costs in larger ports)

TABLE 4.1 **Traffic of main container ports in Spain, 2016 (tons)**

PORT	TOTAL CONTAINER THROUGHPUT	CONTAINER TRANSSHIPMENT	IMPORT-EXPORT VOLUME
Algeciras and Cadiz[a]	55,424,249	50,925,198	4,144,986
Valencia	49,289,732	30,518,642	17,236,240
Barcelona	17,806,952	3,061,426	12,915,128
Bilbao	6,608,117	22,809	5,848,706
Castellón	2,706,931	114,528	2,484,246
Vigo	2,402,495	98,878	1,988,114
Seville	1,270,088	0	124,671
Tarragona	1,610,213	792,427	721,775
Cartagena	1,062,840	1,007	744,337
Gijón	698,595	0	601,726
Total	138,880,212	85,534,915	46,809,928

Source: Puertos del Estado website (http://www.fomento.gob.es/BE/?nivel=2&orden=04000000).
a. The data specify only the province (rather than the port) through which the cargo leaves or enters Spain. Because the province of Cadiz includes two ports (Algeciras and Cadiz), the two ports are grouped together for the analysis.

MAP 4.1
Regions of Spain

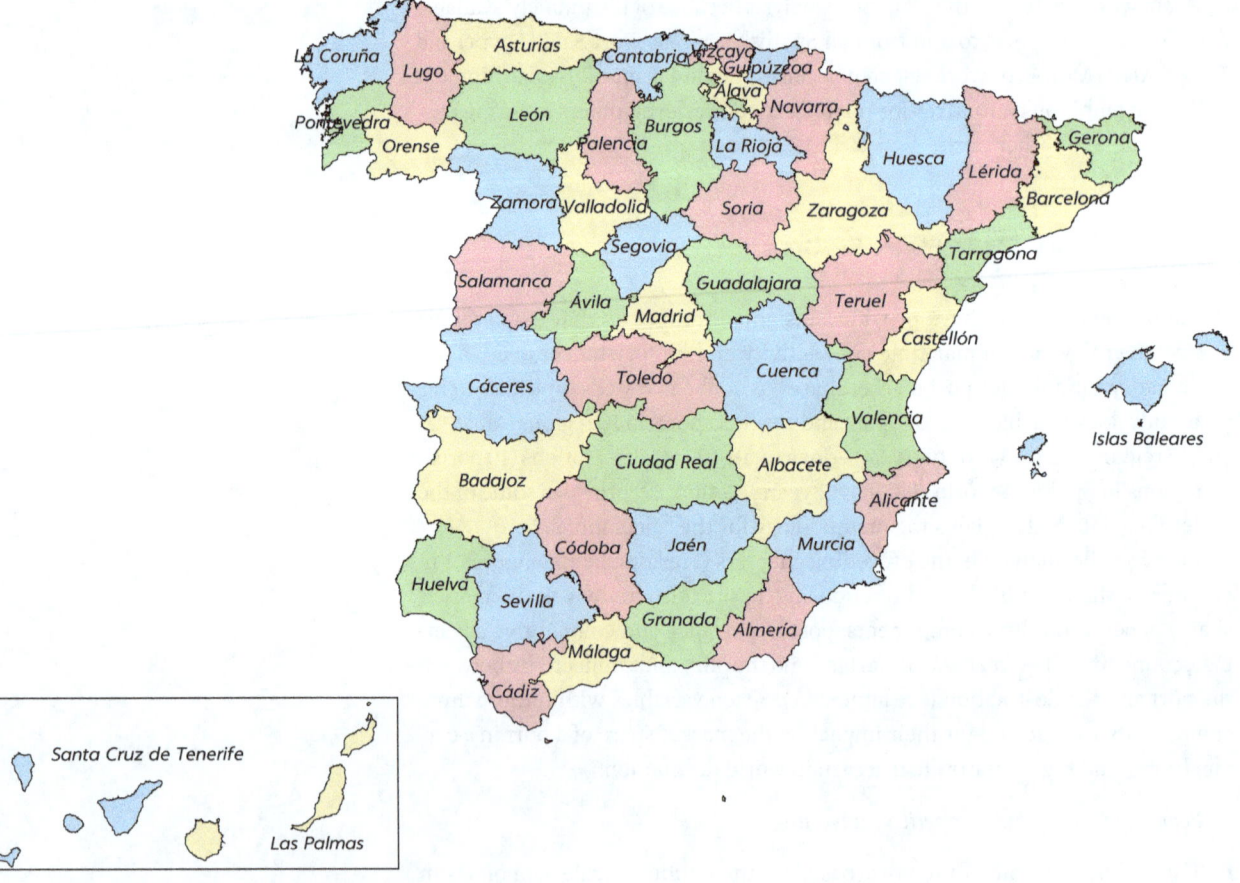

Source: Produced by Emilio Gómez Fernández (https://commons.wikimedia.org/wiki/File:Provincias_de_Espa%C3%B1a.svg).

- Presence of a lock (a dummy variable included because the entrance of the port of Seville has a lock, which affects the maximum size of ships that can enter and the time to reach the port)
- Transshipment orientation (a dummy variable for ports with more than 90 percent transshipment, which includes only Algeciras in Spain).

Connectivity between the hinterland and the port

- Road distance (or log of road distance) to the region relative to the road distance from other ports
- Intermodal connectivity (a dummy variable that indicates whether rail transport connects the port and the hinterland[3]).

Connectivity between the port and the destination

- Maritime distance relative to the maritime distance from other ports
- Maritime connectivity of the port (a function of the number of ship calls and call size).

See table 4.2 for results and annex 4A for details on how the model was estimated.

The main conclusions are:

- Road distance has a significant negative effect on the market share of a port. This is in line with previous studies and is straightforward: the larger the distance, the lower the market share. The relative likelihood of choosing a particular port is halved for every 150 kilometers away it is. This means that hinterlands are highly competitive, with limited overlap
- Maritime distance also influences the market share of a port for a specific world region, which shows that hinterlands are relational. For instance, the share of cargo to and from Asia is higher for Valencia than for other regions of Spain, while the market share of cargo to and from Northern Europe is higher for Bilbao than for other regions of Spain
- Maritime connectivity has a significant positive effect on the market share of a port. The higher the maritime connectivity, the higher the market share

TABLE 4.2 **Subset of coefficients that influence the likelihood of choosing a port**

VARIABLE	DISCRETE CHOICE MODEL REGRESSION				
	ROAD DISTANCE (EXPONENTIAL)	PLUS MARITIME CONNECTIVITY	PLUS MULTIMODAL CONNECTIVITY	ROAD DISTANCE POWER	MARITIME CONNECTIVITY
Pseudo R^2	0.694	0.698	0.699	0.515	0.518
Elasticities of the log of market share (log likelihood) against:					
Road distance to the region relative to the distance from other ports (1,000 kilometers)	−6.04	−6.08	−5.91	—	—
Log of road distance to the region relative to the distance from other ports (1,000 kilometers)	—	—	—	−0.988	−0.991
Intermodal connectivity	—	—	—	0.288	—
Maritime distance relative to the maritime distance from other ports (1,000 kilometers)	—	−0.464	−0.460	—	−0.352
Maritime connectivity of the port	—	0.470	0.477	—	0.336

Source: Calculations based on data from Agencia Tributaria 2017.
Note: — = not available.

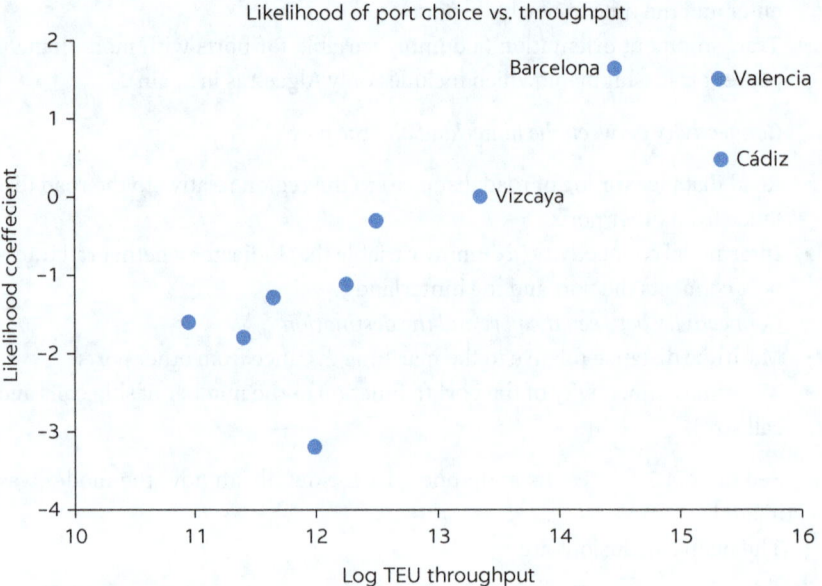

FIGURE 4.1
Likelihood of choosing a port and port throughput

Source: Calculations based on data from Agencia Tributaria 2017.
Note: The data fit the equation likelihood of choice = 0.934 (t = 4.6)$TEUlog$ − 1.35(t = 1.3)TS.

- Valencia appears to reach the most provinces, followed by Barcelona. Other ports in the Mediterranean have no proper hinterland being swallowed by Valencia or Barcelona. Ports on the Atlantic Northwest (Galicia and Basque country) that are further away have their own small hinterlands
- Intermodal connectivity has a significant positive effect on the market share of a port and can increase the likelihood of choosing a port by about 30 percent. The presence of intermodal service increases the market share of that port
- The likelihood of choosing a port at particular location is closely associated with that port's throughput (figure 4.1), with an elasticity close to 1. This result is expected because the likelihood of choosing a port and throughput are necessarily related.

Maritime connectivity has an explanatory value on top of the scale effect (expressed through throughput volume). This is an important insight because connectivity and volume are clearly related, but notwithstanding these relations, maritime connectivity has a significant impact on the market share of a port for traffic between a certain hinterland region and a certain world region. This is because maritime connectivity depends on both the port and world region, and container throughput depends only on the port.

These conclusions generally support policy makers' and port developers' emphasis on maritime and intermodal connectivity, showing that both types of connectivity are important when operators choose a port.

PORT SAID EAST (EGYPT)

This case study shows that maritime connectivity, created through a transshipment hub, does not automatically trigger economic development or complementary development of the port as a national gateway. It focuses on Port Said East, at the entry to the Suez Canal from the Mediterranean, the idea for which emerged in 1998 as a way to take fuller advantage of the roughly 8 percent of global maritime trade and 25 percent of global container movements that pass through the canal. The dual objectives of Port Said East were for it to serve the import and export activities of the contiguous industrial free zone and to meet the expected growth of the Egyptian economy. However, almost 20 years later neither of these objectives has been met, despite Port Said East becoming the largest transshipment port in the Eastern Mediterranean. Port Said East accounted for only about 10 percent of Egypt's containerized international trade in 2012 and thus contributes little to meeting the needs of or stimulating the economy.

Egypt has a comprehensive network of six major container ports serving the hinterland.[4] Port Said East, Port Said West, and Damietta together account for 97 percent of total transshipment volume of the six major container ports (table 4.3) and have a limited role in facilitating trade. The largest ports for import and export are Alexandria, El Dekheila, and Sokhna. The largest contestable hinterland is the Cairo Metropolitan Area.

Data from World Bank (2013b) show that Port Said East has high costs per twenty-foot equivalent unit and per twenty-foot equivalent unit–kilometer—one reason for its low share in container truck traffic to the Cairo Metropolitan Area. And despite being closer to the Cairo Metropolitan Area than most of Egypt's ports (table 4.4), it is on the other side of the canal. The few and inconvenient road and rail crossings of the canal negate some of the distance advantage.

An administrative shortcoming: unaligned development

Port Said East is run as a landlord port. The Suez Canal Container Terminal company is a private joint venture company owned by APM Terminals (55 percent), COSCO (20 percent), Suez Canal & Affiliates (10 percent), the Egyptian private sector (10 percent), and the National Bank of Egypt (5 percent). It operates the three container berths (1,200 meters total length) under a 35-year concession. The Suez Canal Container Terminal company has been fully focused on transshipment since its creation and began handing import–export traffic only

TABLE 4.3 **Traffic of Egyptian ports, 2015**

PORT	TOTAL VOLUME (MILLIONS OF TWENTY-FOOT EQUIVALENT UNITS)	SHARE OF TOTAL VOLUME (%)	TRANSSHIPMENT VOLUME AS A SHARE OF TOTAL PORT VOLUME[a] (%)	SHARE OF TOTAL TRANSSHIPMENT VOLUME[a] (%)	SHARE OF TOTAL IMPORT-EXPORT VOLUME (%)	IMPORT-EXPORT VOLUME (TWENTY-FOOT EQUIVALENT UNITS)
Port Said East	3.60	49	92	74	10	0.29
El Dekheila	0.70	10	6	1	32	0.66
Port Said West	0.80	11	73	13	8	0.22
Alexandria	0.9	12	2	0	28	0.88
Damietta	0.72	10	81	13	5	0.14
Sokhna	0.52	11	11	1	17	0.46
Other	0.12	0	0	n.a.	0	0.12
Total	7.36	100	62	100	100	2.75

Source: Port authority and container terminal operator websites.
Note: n.a. = not applicable.
a. Transshipment containers are counted twice: once at unloading and once at reloading.

TABLE 4.4 **Container truck tariffs from ports to the Cairo metropolitan area, 2013**

PORT	DISTANCE (KILOMETERS)	COST ($ PER TWENTY-FOOT EQUIVALENT UNIT)	COST ($ PER TWENTY-FOOT EQUIVALENT UNIT–KILOMETER)
Port Said East	188	284	1.51
El Dekheila	235	220	0.94
Port Said West	195	195	1.00
Alexandria	230	220	0.96
Damietta	248	275	1.11
Sokhna	145	295	2.03
Average	**206**	**248**	**1.26**

Source: Google Earth; World Bank 2013.

in 2009.[5] In 2014 it handled 250,000 twenty-foot equivalent units of import–export traffic. Egypt's Ministry of Transport does not provide any overall guidance to the ports on what demand they should attract or how they should operate to attract that demand. Port Said East has been operated to maximize its potential its owners and operators rather than to Egypt as a whole. All of Egypt's Mediterranean container terminals have been competing for transshipment demand, and until now, all of them other than Port Said East have been competing for import and export demand.

Supply chain shortcoming: efficient and reliable turnaround

A major hindrance for Port Said East has been that it is inside the Suez Canal Zone, where, until recently, a system of one-way convoys was needed because in some places the canal was too narrow for ships to pass each other. Because vessels often had to wait before or after transshipment to join a convoy, the time to transship containers was longer at Port Said East than at competing ports. The canal has since been widened enough that convoys are no longer needed. In addition, until 2016 Port Said East's access channel to the canal was limited to an eight-hour window each day (because of the convoy system). This hurt transshipment operations as well as import–export operations, which require reliability. Thus Egyptian importers and exporters made little use of the feeder services through Port Said East, and most trade destinations within the region were better connected through the port of Alexandria.

However, a new channel linking Port Said East to the canal opened in 2016, allowing 24-hour access and accommodating the largest container vessels. In addition, an expansion to the canal, completed in 2015, reduced the need for one-way convoys and thus increased capacity and reduced ship waiting and transit times, removing a major barrier for import–export shipping services through Port Said East.

Recent initiatives for integrated development and supply chain efficiency

Formerly complicated governance arrangements changed in 2014 with the establishment of the Suez Canal Economic Zone, which is responsible for developing the whole Suez Canal Corridor, including Port Said East, Port Said West, and the two economic zones in Port Said, with the aim of converting the canal into a development corridor.

The special economic zone adjoining Port Said now has additional incentives, such as relaxed regulations on foreign ownership, fast track visa services, and no import tax on the value added to imports to Egypt. These are aimed make the special economic zone more attractive to value-adding enterprises. Port Said East will also get a dedicated rail freight link to a new technology valley being developed at Ismailia and to a dry port at 10th Ramadan, a large suburb of Cairo. A rail tunnel and two new road tunnels will be built under the canal to avoid the relative isolation of the port and the special economic zone from the Cairo Metropolitan Area. The Suez Canal Economic Zone also plans to develop a new multifeatured residential and industrial community close to the port and special economic zone so that they will not have to depend on commuters from Cairo.

Even if this massive project is only partly successful, the infrastructure links will make Port Said East the most competitive Mediterranean container port for the Cairo hinterland and will shift the development of new economic activity away from the Cairo Metropolitan Area to the Suez Canal Corridor. Taken together the components of the Suez Canal Economic Zone project offer the potential for Port Said East to capture up to 25 percent or more of Egypt's containerized Mediterranean trade.

TANGER MED (MOROCCO)

In 2002 the Moroccan government began a major integrated development project, including a global container port on the Strait of Gibraltar—Tanger Med—with more than 1,000 hectares of industrial and commercial zones and new infrastructure links connecting the port to the national road and rail network. The government's vision was underpinned by three goals:

- Substantially improve Morocco's maritime connectivity with the rest of the world
- Establish a major industrial platform in the Strait of Gibraltar region
- Accelerate the economic and social development of Morocco's northern provinces.

The country's location on the strait in the center of the north–south and east–west shipping routes allows ships to stop without deviating from their route. Tangier sits at the crossing point of some 20 percent of global trade.

Tanger Med began operations in July 2007 and has since evolved into a major Mediterranean hub. The port consists of three main areas: Tanger Med 1, Tanger Med 2, and the passenger port. Tanger Med 1 has a capacity of 3 million twenty-foot equivalent units and 1 million vehicles, in addition to hydrocarbon and dry bulk activity. It has multiple train connections. Tanger Med 2 is a planned extension that will add two deep-water container terminals with capacity for about 6.0 million twenty-foot equivalent units. In 2016 Tanger Med handled almost 3 million twenty-foot equivalent units and was operating at full capacity (TMSA 2016).

At end-2016 Tangier Free Zone directly employed 65,000 people, and the companies operating in the zone had an export turnover of about $4.6 billion a year. Gross domestic product (GDP) in the Tangier region has risen steadily in recent years, from about $7.5 billion in 2009 (8.1 percent of national GDP) to about $8.7 billion in 2013. After an administrative reorganization that added territory to the Tangier region in 2014, GDP in the region was 87 billion dirham (9.4 percent of national GDP). Much of the growth can be traced back to the port. Tangier has seen a steep rise in population in the past few decades, from 250,000 in 1982 to 974,000 in 2016. Morocco's Liner Shipping Connectivity Index value also rose steeply between 2004 and 2016, from 9.39 (2004 = 100) to 64.72, reflecting the added maritime routes.[6] As of 2016, Tanger Med was connected to 169 ports in 68 countries on five continents.[7]

The next section discusses two of the major factors in Tanger Med's success in economic development through enhanced maritime connectivity.

Partnerships and commercial approach

The first factor in Tanger Med's success is government policy, which aimed at aligning a commercial approach to the development of the port, logistics, and industry across all government entities. The government set up the Tanger Med Special Agency, a corporate entity responsible for developing and operating the port and business areas, and granted it public power prerogatives, particularly for territorial management. In line with the commercial approach public–private partnerships were formed with global operators that had strong capabilities in terminal operations. Tanger Med pioneered that approach: for the first time in Morocco port concessions of more than $2 billion were made partly by public entities and partly by private ones.

The Tanger Med Special Agency is fully owned by the government of Morocco. Its institutional and legal setup was molded to fit the needs of the port's objectives. Its range of control encompasses land and other property expropriations. It was thus able to position itself as a one-stop shop to attract investors and support them.[8] Its board includes representatives from the ministries of the interior, finance, equipment, and industry, which has helped align the four departments on strategic decisions. This has been crucial for the mobilization, effectiveness, and coordination of these departments' actions and of the public institutions under their supervision.

The broad mandate of and high-level support for the Tanger Med Special Agency have enabled smooth decision making on building roads, rail links, industrial zones, and towns. The local authorities supported the overall development vision and enabled development by aligning land planning. Financial statements published by the Tanger Med Port Authority show it has achieved revenue growth and healthy profits.[9]

Integrated development

The second factor in Tanger Med's success is its integrated development approach. From the start Tanger Med was not about developing a transshipment facility but about developing a strong economic cluster of freight transport, logistics, and manufacturing activities. The Tangier Free Zone was set up in 1997 under an agreement between the government and a consortium of Moroccan private institutional investors. Their purpose was to ensure the development, construction, and operation of the zone (created under the Free Zones Act). The first industrialists came to Tangier Free Zone in 2000. The law establishing the Tanger Med project in 2002 provided for new industrial, logistics, and commercial free zones in the Strait of Gibraltar region and entrusted the Tanger Med Special Agency with acquiring the land and developing, building on, and operating these areas.

After acquiring land for the zones, the Tanger Med Special Agency decided in 2004 to approach Tangier Free Zone shareholders to discuss an entry into the capital of the Tangier Free Zone. That plan aimed to harmonize the development initiatives of the free zones in the Strait of Gibraltar region and finance and manage the Tangier Free Zone before moving to other zones by capitalizing on the experience with the Tangier Free Zone and enlisting private institutional partners to develop the zones, thus laying the basic orientation to build on public–private partnerships for developing the Tanger Med project. In 2005 the Tanger Med Special Agency became a 51 percent shareholder of the Tangier Free Zone (with institutional shareholders holding the rest).

In 2016 Tanger Med had six industrial zones (table 4.5); the Tanger Med Special Agency decides which companies can set up in the zones, which are managed by Tanger Med Zones (TMSA 2016). The combined developed area covers about 1,200 hectares, and 5,000 hectares are reserved for future use. The zones host more than 700 industrial companies with a yearly export turnover of €5 billion (TMSA 2016). The largest single investor is Renault-Nissan, which has a plant with capacity of 400,000 vehicles.[10] By 2016 cumulative private investment in the zones totaled €2.5 billion (TMSA 2016), 75,000 jobs had been created (with 2,500–5,000 added each year), and some 330 companies were based in the zones. Most companies are from one of five sectors:

- Car manufacturing suppliers (manufacturing cables, car seats, plastics)
- Garment manufacturing and textiles
- Logistics services
- Light manufacturing (shoes, furniture, polymers)
- Various business services (banks, consultancies, industrial cleaning services).

The clustering effect is particularly beneficial to automotive manufacturers, which—even though they source from all over the world—can realize savings by buying heavy items such as car seats within 100 kilometers to save on transport costs. While there is still some automotive industry around Casablanca, experts expect that this will gradually shift to the "golden triangle" of Kénitra, Meknès, and Tangier because roads in Casablanca are congested and production costs are higher (Oxford Business Group 2016).

TABLE 4.5 **Industrial zones in Tanger Med**

ZONE	SURFACE (HECTARES)	SPECIALTY
Tangier Free Zone	400	Automotive, aeronautics, textile
Tangier Automotive City	300	Automotive
Renault Tanger Med	300	Automotive
Tétouan Park	150	Light industrial units, light processing
Logistics Free Zone	100	Logistics
Tétouan Shore	20	Services, offshoring

Source: Tanger Med Zones website (http://www.tangerfreezone.com/map-TFZ/).

Prospects and challenges

Tanger Med's share of Morocco's container import–export flows is 10.3 percent (131,971 twenty-foot equivalent units). Approximately 80 percent of registered container traffic to Morocco is destined for the (essentially industrial) needs of the Tangier–Tétouan region, which reflects the region's share in GDP. Despite double-digit growth in domestic container traffic, Tanger Med's hinterland remains limited to the Tangier region. The largest port in Morocco is Casablanca, but Tangier could gain market share in domestic traffic by directly capturing part of the transshipped traffic and by transporting it overland to its extended hinterland.

Traffic studies have shown that Tanger Med could capture 30 percent of Morocco's domestic container traffic if it had enough rail capacity and an efficient rail system. The competitiveness of the railway refers to the cost of rail transport to Casablanca in comparison with the maritime alternative of feedering. An inland container depot in Casablanca, and possibly in other cities, as well as a body to manage railway traffic (with l'Office National des Chemins de Fer) and operate the dry port is required. The rail connection from Kenitra to Tangier is single track and highly regulated for passenger traffic, which gets priority at junctions, leaving limited capacity for freight trains. The high speed line that is due to open in 2018 should increase capacity on the existing line for more freight trains and pave the way for the construction of an efficient container transport system by rail.

ANNEX 4A: PORT CHOICE: STATISTICAL ANALYSIS OF SPAIN

This annex details the data and methodology used to calculate port market shares in Spain.

DATA

Data on shipments from all Spanish provinces to Spanish seaports—including the volume, value, transport mode (maritime, air, or overland), province of origin, port of departure (if in Spain), and destination country—were obtained from Spain's Tax Agency (Agencia Tributaria). A database was then constructed that divided all maritime shipments according to departure and destination region. The number of observations was determined by the number of peninsular provinces in Spain—that is, 47—thus excluding the Balearic Islands, the Canary Islands, Ceuta, and Melilla; by the number of Spanish peninsular ports that handle containers; and by the number of destination country regions. Destination country regions were one of four world regions, essentially covering the areas north, east, south, and west of Spain. This grouping makes sense because the differences in distances to the regions are the same for all destinations in the regions: Valencia (Spain) is about 300 kilometers closer than Algeciras (Spain) to any destination to the east, whether it is Mumbai, Piraeus, Shanghai, or Taranto (Italy). Trade with Andorra and Portugal was excluded because both countries could not be classified into one of the four world regions.

The 11 Spanish peninsular ports that handle substantial container traffic are Algeciras, Barcelona, Bilbao, Cadiz Cartagena, Castellón, Gijón, Seville,

Tarragona, Valencia, and Vigo. The data specify only the province (rather than the port) through which the cargo leaves or enter Spain. Because the province of Cadiz includes two ports with high container traffic (Algeciras and Cadiz), the two ports are grouped together for the analysis.

Because the model was developed for containerized trade,[11] shipments that are bulk or roll-on, roll-off need to be excluded. But the data do not include information on how the goods are shipped, so the largest shipments and shipments with the lowest value per ton (both of which are more likely to be bulk) were excluded,[12] as were shipments to typical roll-on, roll-off destinations from Spain (France, Italy, and Morocco).

Formalization of port choice: a shipper perspective

The choice is that of a trader located in a city or administrative division i (such as provinces, in the case of Spain) trading with world destination k through the port gateway j. The probability that a trader in i uses port gateway j when trading with region k is P_j^{ik}. By construction the total of probability is one for each origin-destination pair (i,j): $\sum_j P_j^{ik} = 1$. Discrete choice models posit a multinomial logit form by which $P_j^{ik} \propto e^{U_j^{jk}}$ likelihood of choice is loglinear), where U_j^{ik} is the utility of choosing gateway j for an operator in i trading with destination k. By the normalization condition for the choices available in (i,k): $P_j^{ik} = \dfrac{e^{U_j^{jk}}}{\sum_l e^{U_l^{jk}}}$. Following the conceptual framework of connectivity introduced in figure 1.1 in chapter 1, the utility of choosing gateway j for an operator in i trading with destination k is a function of three contributions: $U_j^{kj} = U_j^1 + U_{ij}^2 + U_{kj}^3$.

- **Portance of gateway j or competitive advantage compared with the other ports.** This component depends on such variables as shipping connectivity, throughput, and port productivity of the port (with some serious risk of collinearity among those variables):

  $U_j^1 = \beta_1 \text{connectivity variables of gateway } j$

  This component of utility can be a gateway fixed effect (dummy variable) that reveals the importance of the port, or it can be a direct series of port indicators.

- **Interaction between origin i and gateway j or connectivity between the hinterland and port.** This component encompasses variables that measure the accessibility of gateway j from origin i such as distance (or log distance) or existence of intermodal connectivity.

$U_{ij}^2 = \beta_2 \text{accessibiliy or connectivity variable for the link from an operator in } i \text{ to gateway } j$

- **Interaction or bilateral connectivity between gateway j and destination k.** This component captures the relative connectivity or proximity advantage of gateway j for shipping to and from destination k through difference in shipping distance and indicators of shipping connectivity for the destination (existence of service, frequency, and the like):

$U_{kj}^3 = \beta_3 \text{connectivity advantage of gateway } j \text{ when trading with destination } k$

The coefficients βs are to be estimated. The discrete choice models is estimated using a Poisson regression applied to the value of frequencies and using fixed effects for origin-destination pairs.

Explanatory variables

The explanatory variables in table 4.2 in the main text are in line with previous studies on port choice (Anderson, Opaluch, and Grigalunas 2009; De Langen 2007; Ferrari, Parola, and Gattorna 2011; Halim, Kwakkel, and Tavasszy 2016; Luo and Grigalunas 2003; Malchow and Kanafani 2004; Tavasszy et al. 2011; Tongzon 2009; Veldman, Garcia-Alonso, and Vallejo-Pinto 2011).

Port importance and competitive advantage

Throughput volume is the total throughput volume of the port, based on the idea that there are scale economies in port operations, leading to higher productivity and lower costs in larger ports. The dummy variable for the presence of a lock was included because the entrance of the port of Seville is constrained by a lock that affects both the maximum size of ships that can enter and the time to reach the port.

The transshipment orientation variable is based partly on the results from the case study of Malta in chapter 3. It tests whether having more than 90 percent transshipment traffic negatively affects a port's shares in hinterland regions. The theoretical logic is that if both shipping companies and the terminal operator are focused on transshipment operations, this is (somewhat) at the expense of services for containers to and from the hinterland, because the terminal is not designed for such flows and shipping companies give priority to efficient transshipment operations. In the analysis for Spain, Algeciras is the only port with a transshipment orientation (92 percent of traffic is transshipment). The dummy variable takes the value 1 for transshipment-oriented ports and 0 otherwise.

Connectivity between the hinterland and the port

Road distance is the additional road distance between port p and hinterland h in kilometers, relative to the road distance from hinterland h to its nearest port. The data are calculated for all provinces and to all ports using Google maps. The distance is calculated from each port to the provincial capital city, where the main density of population and economic activity is concentrated. For a port located in the capital city of a province, a distance of 50 kilometers was used.

Intermodal connectivity—a dummy variable indicating the existence of intermodal connectivity between port p and hinterland h—is calculated based on data on intermodal connections in a matrix of 47 regions and 10 ports. It has the value 1 if there is an intermodal connection and 0 otherwise.[13] The number of intermodal connections is limited. Table 4A.1 shows the intermodal connectivity of the port of Algeciras (Spain) as an example.

Connectivity between the port and the destination

Maritime distance is the additional maritime distance between port p and a world region in nautical miles, relative to the maritime distance from the world region to the closest Spanish port. The relative distances may matter because a shorter route would save time and generalized transport costs. The relative distances are calculated by taking one reference port[14] and collecting data on distance to this port through the Sea-Distances.org website (https://sea-distances.org).

TABLE 4A.1 **Intermodal connectivity of the port of Algeciras (Spain), 2016**

PROVINCE	INTERMODAL CONNECTIVITY	PROVINCE	INTERMODAL CONNECTIVITY	PROVINCE	INTERMODAL CONNECTIVITY
Alava	0	Guadalajara	0	Palencia	0
Albacete	0	Guipuzcoa	0	Pontevedra	0
Alicante	0	Huelva	0	Salamanca	0
Almeria	0	Huesca	0	Santander	0
Avila	0	Jaen	0	Segovia	0
Badajoz	0	La Coruña	0	Seville	1
Barcelona	0	La Rioja	0	Soria	0
Burgos	0	Leon	0	Tarragona	0
Caceres	0	Lleida	0	Teruel	0
Cadiz	0	Lugo	0	Toledo	0
Castellon	0	Madrid	1	Valencia	0
Ciudad Real	0	Malaga	1	Valladolid	0
Cordoba	1	Murcia	0	Vizcaya	0
Cuenca	0	Navarra	0	Zamora	0
Girona	0	Ourense	0	Zaragoza	0
Granada	1	Oviedo	0		

Source: Calculations based on data from the Intermodal Links website (www.intermodallinks.com) and the Autoridad Portuaria de la Bahía de Algeciras website (http://www.apba.es/ferrocarril).

TABLE 4A.2 **Distances in nautical miles from Spanish ports to four main world regions**

PORT	EASTERN MEDITERRANEAN AND ASIA	NORTHERN AND CENTRAL EUROPE	NORTH AND CENTRAL AMERICA	WEST AFRICA AND SOUTH AMERICA
Algeciras	327	631	219	0
Barcelona	0	1,142	730	511
Bilbao	1,186	37	233	573
Cartagena	108	864	452	233
Castellon	72	1,037	625	406
Gijón	1,063	0	108	450
Seville	454	610	202	44
Tarragona	34	1,108	696	477
Valencia	81	1,014	602	383
Vigo	842	136	0	238

Source: Calculations based on data from the Sea-Distances.org website (https://sea-distances.org).

Table 4A.2 shows the relative distances in nautical miles from the 10 Spanish ports to the four world regions.

Maritime connectivity of port p with a certain world region is a complicated variable. Based on data drawing on Lloyd's List Intelligence ship movements (see chapter 2), maritime connectivity is expressed as the sum of the capacities of container ships that have called in port p and also in the world region in question. However, because absolute connectivity is not of interest, the values were normalized with a score of 100 for the best-connected Spanish port.

Results

Eight variations of the discrete choice model regression were estimated. All included the port as a fixed effect. The variations included different combinations of variables on connectivity between the hinterland and the port and on connectivity between the port and the destination (table 4A.3).

The dummy variable for the likelihood of choosing a port is highly correlated with the throughput of the port (see figure 4.1) because a bigger port attracts more traffic and expands its hinterland. A downward correction is needed for Cádiz, because the port of Algeciras, Spain, is primarily a transshipment port.

The likelihood of choosing a port depends on the distance to the hinterland destination. This dependence is tested with an exponential function (models 2, 4, 6, 7, and 8 in table 4A.3) or a power dependence (models 3 and 5 in table 4A.3). The exponential models have a substantially better fit (pseudo R^2 in table 4A.3). The exponent in the power dependence is very close to −1, which is exactly the

TABLE 4A.3 **Estimation of the port choice model for Spain**

VARIABLE	DISCRETE CHOICE MODEL REGRESSION							
	1	2	3	4	5	6	7	8
Number of observations	3,760	3,760	3,760	3,760	3,760	3,760	3,760	3,760
Pseudo R^2	0.334	0.694	0.515	0.698	0.518	0.698	0.695	0.699
Port importance or competitive advantage (dummy variable)								
Barcelona	0.311	1.64	1.13	1.45	1.00	1.69	1.25	1.34
Cadiz	−0.087	0.474	0.470	0.040	0.158	0.398	−0.130	−0.056
Castellon	−2.00	−1.12	−1.76	−1.09	−1.75	−1.09	−1.13	−1.11
Murcia	−2.52	−1.79	−1.84	−1.80	−1.84	−1.82	−1.78	−1.87
Oviedo	−1.52	−1.60	−1.87	−1.63	−1.89	−1.64	−1.59	−1.61
Pontevedra	−0.467	−0.310	0.347	−0.393	0.287	−0.388	−0.328	−0.454
Seville	−3.23	−3.20	−2.60	−3.25	−2.630	−3.26	−3.12	−3.22
Tarragona	−2.31	−1.29	−1.68	−1.25	−1.66	−1.24	−1.30	−1.26
Valencia	0.878	1.50	1.46	1.10	1.17	1.52	0.801	1.07
Vizcaya	0 (reference port)							
Connectivity between the hinterland and the port								
Road distance to the region relative to the distance from other ports (1,000 kilometers)	—	−6.04	—	−6.08	—	−6.08	−6.05	−5.91
Log of road distance to the region relative to the distance from other ports (1,000 kilometers)	—	—	−0.988	—	−0.991	—	—	—
Intermodal connectivity	—	—	—	—	—	—	—	0.2879
Connectivity between the port and the destination								
Maritime distance relative to the maritime distance from other ports (1,000 kilometers)	—	—	—	−0.464	−0.352	−0.504	—	−0.460
Maritime connectivity of the port	—	—	—	0.470	0.337	—	0.776	0.477

Source: Calculations based on data from Agencia Tributaria 2017.
Note: All coefficients are highly significant; — = not available.

classical gravity specification (inverse of distance) used to estimate market potential of an economic center in economic geography.

The dampening effect of distance on likelihood of choosing a gateway is rather strong. In the exponential formula the coefficient for distance (in thousands of kilometers) is about minus 6, meaning that the likelihood of choosing a port is halved for every additional 150 kilometers of road distance. The overlap between the hinterlands is thus quite limited, or the hinterlands are relatively well defined. It is very possible that the values observed are specific to Spain and cannot be extrapolated to bigger countries where transportation happens at a larger scale.

Intermodal connectivity improves the likelihood of choosing a port by about 30 percent (corresponding to the coefficient in model 8). This is sizeable effect but not as strong as the impact of distance.

Both maritime distance relative to the maritime distance from other ports and maritime connectivity of the port have a significant effect on the likelihood of choosing a port, though the effect is not as large as road distance to the region relative to the distance from other ports. The signs are as expected. An additional 1,000 kilometers in relative distance to the destination reduces the likelihood of choosing a port by a third.

NOTES

1. In addition, because of Spain's geography, the vast majority of the country's exports use a Spanish port, which makes a statistical analysis viable.
2. Another model included the productivity of Spanish ports (reported by the *Journal of Commerce* and IHS Markit) as a variable. However, the results were counterintuitive, probably because the data were imperfect, and available for only nine ports.
3. Only rail transport connections were considered because Spain has no inland waterways for containers.
4. These are the ports managed by the four port authorities. There are some other privately operated bulk ports.
5. An import–export container is one that enters Egyptian national territory (including special economic zones and dry ports). It excludes transshipment containers.
6. The underlying data come from Containerisation International and are http://unctadstat.unctad.org/wds/TableViewer/tableView.aspx?ReportId=92.
7. *Tanger Med News*, April 2016, p. 2.
8. All information in this paragraph is from TMSA (2016).
9. See www.ammc.ma.
10. Based on data from the Tanger Med Port Authority website (http://www.tmpa.ma/en/activites-services/activite-vehicules/).
11. Port choices for containerized trade differ from those of bulk commodities. For instance, maritime and intermodal connectivity are not relevant for bulk shipping.
12. Given that container throughput from the Puertos del Estado website (http://www.fomento.gob.es/BE/?nivel=2&orden=04000000) includes data on container tare weight and empty containers, import–export cargo was removed until the total volume averaged 85 percent of the published container throughput.
13. This method is imperfect. First, one could argue that a province is also intermodally connected when there is a service from a neighboring region to a port. In addition, it does not consider the link quality; regardless of the capacity or frequency, the score for a connection is 1. However, given the complexity of including such indirect intermodal connections, this issue remains unaddressed here.
14. The reference port for each of the four world regions is Amsterdam for Northern Europe, Port Said for Eastern Mediterranean and Asia, Abidjan for West Africa and South America, and Houston for North and Central America.

REFERENCES

Agencia Tributaria. 2017. "Flujo de Importación y Exportación." Madrid. http://www
.agenciatributaria.es/AEAT.internet/Inicio/La_Agencia_Tributaria/Memorias_y
_estadisticas_tributarias/Estadisticas/Comercio_exterior/Datos_estadisticos/Descarga
_de_Datos_Estadisticos/Descarga_de_datos_anuales_territoriales_en_Euros__Centimos
_/Descarga_de_datos_anuales_territoriales_en_Euros__Centimos_.shtml.

Anderson, C. M., J. J. Opaluch, and T. A. Grigalunas. 2009. "The Demand for Import Services at US Container Ports." *Maritime Economics & Logistics* 11 (2): 156–85.

De Langen, P. W. 2007. "Port Competition and Selection in Contestable Hinterlands: The Case of Austria." *European Journal of Transport and Infrastructure Research* 7 (1): 1–14.

Ferrari, C., F. Parola, and E. Gattorna. 2011. "Measuring the Quality of Port Hinterland Accessibility: The Ligurian Case." *Transport Policy* 18 (2): 382–91.

Halim, R. A., J. H. Kwakkel, and L. A. Tavasszy. 2016. "A Strategic Model of Port-Hinterland Freight Distribution Networks." *Transportation Research Part E: Logistics and Transportation Review* 95: 368–84.

Luo, M., and T. A. Grigalunas. 2003. "A Spatial-Economic Multimodal Transportation Simulation Model for US Coastal Container Ports." *Maritime Economics & Logistics* 5 (2): 158–78.

Malchow, M. B., and A. Kanafani. 2004. "A Disaggregate Analysis of Port Selection." *Transportation Research Part E: Logistics and Transportation Review* 40 (4): 317–37.

Oxford Business Group. 2016. *The Report: Morocco 2016*. London.

Tavasszy, L., M. Minderhoud, J. F. Perrin, and T. Notteboom. 2011. "A Strategic Network Choice Model for Global Container Flows: Specification, Estimation and Application." *Journal of Transport Geography* 19 (6): 1163–72.

TMSA (Tanger Med Special Agency). 2016. "Tanger Med Port, The New Mediterranean Strategic Hub." Oued Rmel, Morocco. http://www.tmpa.ma/wp-content/uploads/2016/12/Brochure-TMPA-en-Anglais.pdf.

Tongzon, J. L. 2009. "Port Choice and Freight Forwarders." *Transportation Research Part E: Logistics and Transportation Review* 45 (1): 186–95.

Veldman, S., L. Garcia-Alonso, and J. A. Vallejo-Pinto. 2011. "Determinants of Container Port Choice in Spain." *Maritime Policy and Management* 38 (5): 509–22.

World Bank. 2013a. *Doing Business in Egypt 2014: Understanding Regulations for Small and Medium-Size Enterprises*. Washington, DC.

———. 2013b. *Doing Business: Trading Across Borders: Egypt*. Washington, DC.

5 Enhancing Connectivity and Port Development Strategies

The case studies show that the development of ports and hinterlands depends on context, past patterns, or path dependence. Despite these idiosyncrasies, it is tempting to identify a typology of connectivity patterns and the dynamic of changes behind the transition from one connectivity pattern to another. Such a double typology could inform policy makers who are developing policies and strategies to improve connectivity.

This chapter takes the perspective of the agency in charge of a port. These agencies have a dual responsibility: their primary responsibility is the development of the port and its related facilities as a commercial business, but they are also concerned with the economic development of the hinterland. This chapter tries to reconcile a vision for port expansion strategies with a more static perspective looking at connectivity patterns and geographical typology of places.

The first section theorizes different strategies of port expansion and how they create an evolutionary dynamic that influences the development of a port's hinterland. The second section proposes a typology of connectivity patterns for a set of port-hinterland combinations. The final section presents examples of patterns and evolutionary strategies from the Mediterranean.

PORT DEVELOPMENT STRATEGY AND HINTERLAND DYNAMIC

Given the economic benefits of better connectivity for port users and for society at large, policy makers, port managers, and shipping companies are all active in policies and strategies to improve connectivity. The three sets of actors contribute through different but interrelated mechanisms to increasing a port's attractiveness and its throughput.

From a commercial perspective, there are three markets that a port can serve: transshipment,[1] the hinterland, and a local captive cargo base. The first two markets are very competitive because expanding them requires attracting services (in the case of transshipment) or demand (in the case of hinterland) from other ports. Competition for the captive cargo base is much weaker, and a port development strategy focused on the captive cargo base usually tries to generate new demand rather than attracting it from other ports. The size of a captive cargo base depends mostly on the extent to which the port has developed into a logistics and manufacturing cluster and on the population and economic activity of the port city or metropolitan area.[2]

The three markets are interrelated—as are the strategies for port development that relate to each. An existing strength in one market can serve as a platform for expanding the others. For example, more maritime connectivity from transshipment is a platform to expand the hinterland but requires infrastructure and services (figure 5.1). An expanded hinterland or captive cargo base turns a port into a must-call destination. A port with a suitable location in maritime networks and decent capacity and terminal productivity can attract transshipment flows. Better overseas and hinterland connectivity increases the attractiveness of a port for logistics and manufacturing activities, which also require the location to have solid fiscal performance, a strong labor market, and high scores for ease of doing business. A strong captive cargo base provides a basis for expanding the hinterland. Flows directly to the hinterland can be combined with flows generated by local logistics and manufacturing activities. This creates scale economies, especially when rail or barge transport is used. In addition, the economic benefits of infrastructure that connects the port to the hinterland are larger when that infrastructure is used both for transit cargo and for cargo related to local logistics and manufacturing activities.

Port development can be based on any or all of the markets, but the time frames are different. Transshipment flows can be attracted relatively quickly because shipping companies can shift traffic from one port to another without major infrastructure investments (beyond a container terminal with enough storage space). Transshipment is rather footloose, especially given the intense competition among numerous hub ports in the Mediterranean. So ports can attract traffic in a short time span but can also lose it in a short time span. A partnership in which a shipping company takes a substantial share of investment in port infrastructure can reduce this volatility.

In contrast, expanding the hinterland generally requires investment in road and rail infrastructure (and in inland waterways for some ports) and thus takes

FIGURE 5.1

Three port development paths and strategies

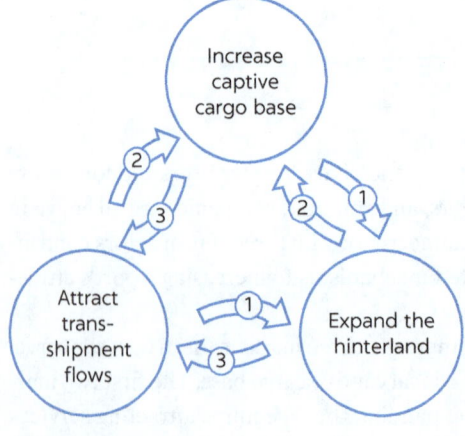

1. **Hinterland expands,** with more maritime connectivity, from transshipment activity and/or when inland destination benefits from the economies of scale of a strong captive cargo base.
2. **Captive cargo increases** as better maritime and hinterland connectivity expand the market potential of logistics and production activity in the port vicinity.
3. **Transshipment develops** as hinterland and/or captive cargo activities expand because the port becomes more attractive to call at for shipping lines.

Note: Does not include non-port-related interventions such as investment in maritime safety and security, which also improves connectivity.

longer to increase connectivity than attracting transshipment traffic does. These investments are generally time-consuming to plan and implement. In addition, hinterland port traffic does not shift spontaneously or instantaneously: existing supply chains often persist, because switching entails costs.

Similarly, expanding the captive cargo base is a lengthy process because it requires developing land for logistics and manufacturing and attracting customers to lease or buy that land. Many ports that start from a local cargo base are in the downtown area of a port city, where land for expansion is scarce or expensive. Only after the investment in attractive sites for logistics and manufacturing is realized will logistics and manufacturing operations attract additional traffic.

A TYPOLOGY OF PORTS BY CONNECTIVITY AND DEVELOPMENT STRATEGY

Another key takeaway from the case studies is the path- and place-dependency of ports. Not every coastal village can evolve into a major port metropolis, and even the largest and best-established local cargo-based ports may see a decrease in market share because of fierce competition in both maritime networks and the hinterlands.

Figure 5.2 provides a typology of ports based on hinterland connectivity and shipping connectivity. Growing one or both dimensions will increase traffic (indicated by the size of the circle in the center). A port's starting point greatly influences the past and current operation and trade facilitation of the port and the success of the port's plans and strategies. Cell A represents a typical cargo-based port, with a short hinterland connection (indicated by the dotted line in the left of the cell) and only direct maritime services to other ports, some of which are feeder services to hub ports (indicated by the dotted line in the right of the cell). The vertical axis indicates the importance of hinterland connectivity in a development strategy, and the horizontal axis indicates the importance of maritime connectivity in a development strategy.

Path A→B2→C3 in figure 5.2 shows a development strategy focused exclusively on transshipment, with maritime service evolving from direct and feeder services (A) to one with some transshipment (B2) to one with transshipment and its own feeder services (C3). Path A→B1→C1 shows a development path focused exclusively on hinterland connectivity (including the cargo base), with the hinterland evolving from a minor port with limited hinterland and maritime connectivity (A) to an expanded cargo base (B1, with a heavier land connectivity line) to expansion in the hinterland beyond the cargo base (C1).

A port that already has a cargo base (B1 in figure 5.2) and aims to develop transshipment service would add some transshipment services (C2) and ultimately have a stronger cargo base and more balanced demand (D2) than a pure transshipment port.

A pure transshipment port (C3 in figure 5.2) that focused on hinterland development would move from D2 to E, thereby reinforcing its hinterland connectivity while maintaining high maritime connectivity. Conversely, a pure cargo base and hinterland port (C1) that focused on transshipment would attract deep-sea services or direct calls (D1) then move to transshipment to become a fully-fledged and dominant node (E).

Ports that specialize in one of the two dimensions could face unbalanced demand because demand is based only on cargo (B1 in figure 5.2) or maritime

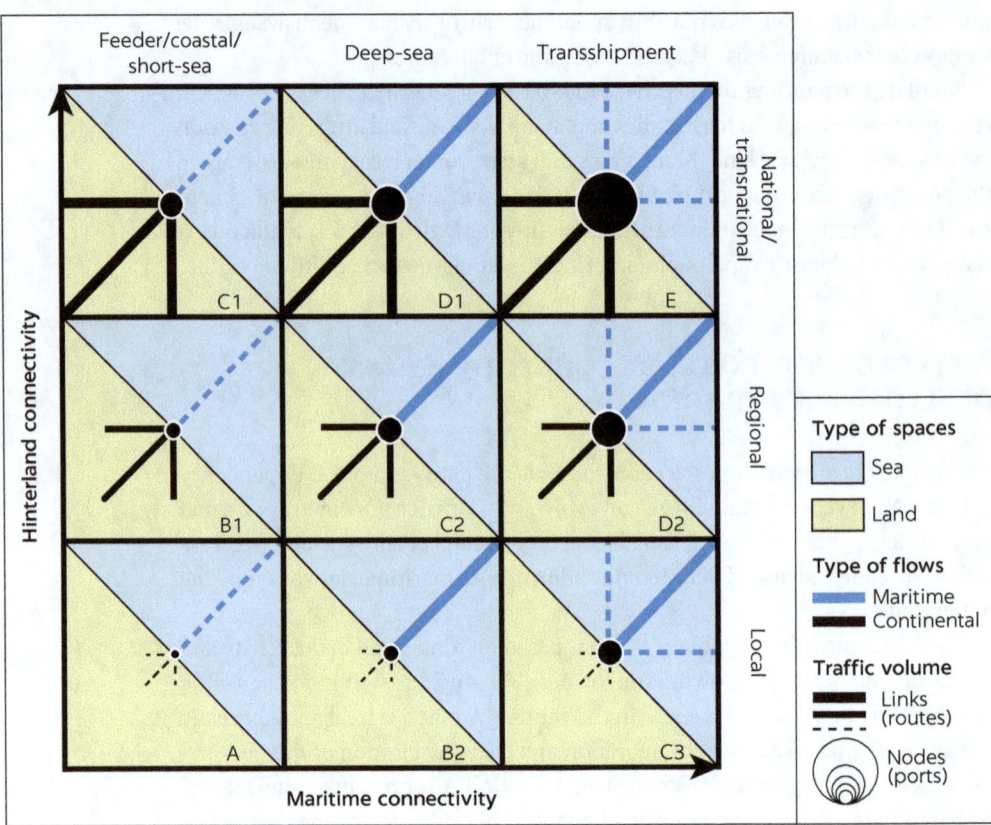

FIGURE 5.2
Typology of port connectivity

traffic (B2 and C3). Ports with less specialization (C2, D1, and D2) face more balanced demand and are therefore less vulnerable to traffic shifts and port competition.

PATTERNS OF PORT DEVELOPMENT AND EVOLUTIONARY STRATEGIES IN THE MEDITERRANEAN

The ports in the Mediterranean constitutes a rich set of examples of the typologies in figure 5.2. Many of these ports have evolved from one typology to another by following the development paths and strategies in figure 5.1.

The transshipment hub strategy

The transshipment hub strategy aims at first becoming a maritime hub and to use the hub position as a platform to expand the hinterland and local cargo base (path A→B2→C3→D2→E in figure 5.2). This strategy entails investing mainly in maritime connectivity and port efficiency first and rarely creates local or national socioeconomic benefits or enhances trade. Industry links with the local or national economy are often limited, especially when it comes to attracting value-added activities such as storage, warehousing, and related logistical activities onsite.

Slack and Gouvernal (2015, p. 406) concluded that, with a few exceptions (such as Dubai and Singapore), transshipment hubs have limited local impacts because of "long-term uncertainty of shipping services to transshipment hubs, the costs of stripping containers in hub ports with no scale advantages, the distance from major markets, and the limited volume of actual goods available in most hubs." In line with this conclusion, Ducruet, Itoh and Joly (2015) showed that most of the southern EU transshipment hubs have below-average productivity (regional GDP) and higher unemployment rates than their national averages. Examples abound in the Mediterranean: Algeciras (Spain), Cagliari (Italy), Gioia Tauro (Italy), Sines (Portugal), and Taranto (Italy), all of which developed as growth poles by the central government aimed at creating regional balance based on the establishment of a heavy industrial complex in the 1970s. The exception might be Tangier (Morocco).

Without investment in hinterland connectivity, attracting transshipment functions (that is, going from B2 to C3 in figure 5.2) may not have the expected effect of transforming the regional economy. Most transshipment hubs in the Mediterranean are located near the trunk line on islands or peninsulas and thus have limited hinterland connectivity. Some achieved a hinterland expansion strategy following the attraction of transshipment activities (path A→B2→C3→D2). For instance, Sines (Portugal) attracted the global terminal operator Port of Singapore Authority in 2004, but its traffic and hinterland penetration started to grow substantially only 10 years later because of competition from existing gateways and hubs. Algeciras (Spain) showed a similar trajectory, with more and more traffic (trucking) serving the capital city and core economic center Madrid.

In addition, given the competition between ports for hub status, the hub-only development strategy is risky. For instance, attracting the global terminal operator DP World in Djen Djen (Algeria) did not produce the expected economic impacts mainly because of limited hinterland accessibility and competition from existing hubs (Mohamed-Chérif and Ducruet 2011). Djen Djen has progressed from A to only C2 in figure 1.2. Failure can be worse, even with a much favorable location, as seen when Crete's local population rejected a new container terminal at Timbaki because of environmental and landscape concerns and limited socioeconomic impact.[3] In the case of the Enfidha project (Tunisia), the ambition is to shift from A to E, which may be difficult, especially under an unfavorable political context.

One attractive development path is to use transshipment traffic to develop a logistics and manufacturing cluster (C3→D2 in figure 5.2). The new port and industrial free zone in Tanger Med (Morocco) was able to do this (see case studies in chapters 3 and 4 and Ducruet, Mohamed-Chérif, and Cherfaoui 2011). Its success came not only from being able to attract major shipping lines and terminal operators, but also from having an integrated project by the government to alleviate the poorer socioeconomic conditions in the Tangier-Tétouan region. In comparison, Malta Freeport has remained at C3, while Tangier has already reached D2 and is contemplating further progress to E through increased hinterland connectivity and value-added activities.

Several well-established ports that were already important gateways have also attempted a strategy of development through transshipment. Piraeus attracted the global terminal operator COSCO in 2008 to achieve such a goal, but Valencia (Spain) pursued a favorable national port policy to support trade activities. This corresponds to the path D1→E or C2→D2 in figure 5.2, depending on the amplitude of connectivity, with the risk of congestion and lack of space for further expansion. Bejaia has not yet developed into a transshipment hub, but it attracted both the Singaporean operator Protek and new short-sea lines to expand its maritime connectivity (A→B2). Other positive factors in Bejaia's development were the fact that it is a relatively large city away from Algiers, that its hinterland was not very accessible to competitors until recently, and that its port authority had a proactive attitude toward development. By contrast, most other important port cities and gateways in the Mediterranean have not adopted a transshipment strategy because they are self-contained markets with low hinterland connectivity (B1), especially those southern Mediterranean ports. The large gateways of the northern Mediterranean are too far from the trunk line to be attractive for transshipment activities, despite their strong cargo base and hinterland connectivity.

The hinterland expansion strategy

A second strategy tries to make a port reach more-extensive hinterlands (B1→C1 in figure 5.2). This strategy places intermodal connectivity center stage because distant hinterlands are increasingly served through intermodal services (rail or barge). Genoa and Marseilles are examples of Mediterranean ports that have followed this strategy. Ports that expand their hinterland provide shipping companies access to larger volumes and thus can become must-call ports. They may also attract large shipping flows through direct intercontinental services. Being a must-call port provides a sound basis for attracting transshipment traffic. Perhaps the best examples of this path are Antwerp and Hamburg (both E), which have attracted substantial transshipment traffic despite their upstream locations.

Other successful examples are Piraeus, a self-contained market and the largest and capital city of Greece, and Valencia (Spain), a gateway to Madrid. Both handle substantial transshipment traffic—well above 60 percent in the case of Piraeus. In the same way that extensive hinterland traffic provides a platform for attracting transshipment, it also provides a platform for expanding the logistics and manufacturing cluster. However, attracting logistics and (downstream) manufacturing requires location attractiveness beyond maritime and hinterland connectivity (see Ferrari, Parola, and Morchio 2006). Especially relevant are administrative procedures (such as customs), quality and flexibility of the labor market, and possible benefits of co-location. In this sense, agglomeration effects tend to favor ports with established logistics and manufacturing clusters. But the respective hinterlands of Piraeus and Valencia remain local or national, so that these ports tend to remain at D2 in figure 5.2.

Despite limited potential for hinterland connectivity—which is due to the concentration of population and markets near the coast—some non-EU Mediterranean ports have adopted a regionalization strategy (Notteboom and Rodrigue 2005). Algiers is one example: it developed suburban dry ports at Rouiba to avoid congestion in the urban core. But Algiers's parallel transshipment strategy did not yield the expected effects, though it did attract DP World. Today, most of Algeria's trade is transshipped through Marsaxlokk (Malta) and Tangier (Morocco), similar to how many other large cities with limited hinterland connectivity are served by feeder vessels (B1 in figure 5.2). Although Serbia has access to shipping by river, it is otherwise a landlocked country served by competing ports—Bar (Montenegro), Dubrovnik (Croatia), and Thessaloniki (Greece)—which have expanded their hinterland connectivity to try to catch this market. Tangier (Morocco) has a hinterland expansion strategy on the agenda, but Morocco's core markets are better served by Casablanca. Tanger Med (Morocco) is expanding its hinterland, attracting (current and new) traffic that would otherwise go Casablanca.

Several EU ports have expanded their hinterland connectivity, backed by a well-established cargo base (Barcelona), even beyond national borders (Koper, Slovenia, and Trieste, Italy, with Austria), but without expanding their transshipment activities for the same reasons cited above. Such a trajectory is a shift from a balanced and self-sufficient gateway (C2 in figure 5.2) to a more transnational gateway (D1).

The cargo base expansion strategy

The third strategy is based on development of and then from a strong local cargo base. Such development may come partly from logistics and manufacturing activities and partly from the population and economic size of the port metropolitan area. Ports that follow this strategy include Alexandria, Barcelona, Izmir, Naples, and Radès, which were built mainly for local needs. For Barcelona the captive regional market is very important and may play a role in making infrastructure investments viable. For instance, the rail connections with the strong logistics cluster in Zaragoza have developed because of the combination of import–export cargo and domestic cargo between Barcelona and Zaragoza (Van den Berg and de Langen 2011).

However, building a local cargo base from scratch is an uphill initiative. Tunisia's Enfidha multifunctional complex, which was intended to comprise a new international airport, container port, and free trade zone, has not materialized for financial and political reasons (the latter being the Arab Spring). It was located far from the closest market centers and from the trunk line; only the airport, which focused on tourism rather than cargo, was completed. By contrast, Sohar (Oman) was more successful after receiving large investments from domestic state-owned enterprises. The investments created agglomeration effects that triggered a huge inflow of foreign direct investment to Sohar.

Government intervention and attraction of terminal operators may not increase shipping connectivity but can have enormous effects in value-added activities, as in Mersin (Turkey) under the PSA/Akfen consortium since 2007 (Merk and Bagis 2013). Competition for hinterlands among southern Turkish ports is fierce, but Mersin's hinterland remains mainly captive and local, despite some flows up to 300 kilometers away and a small portion towards Irak. Mersin remains a medium-size port with limited hinterland and maritime connectivity but with strong industrial links between the port and the local economy.

NOTES

1. This market can be further segmented into interlining (transfer of containers between mother vessels at the crossroads of the trunk line) and hub-and-spoke (transfer of containers between mother vessels and feeder ships within the region).
2. The size of the port city is also influenced by the extent to which the port develops as a logistics and manufacturing cluster, especially in developing countries. A well-developed cluster is an important agglomeration force for the growth of the urban region (see Fujita and Mori 1996 and Slack and Gouvernal 2015).
3. See http://archive.li/Go8VC.

REFERENCES

Ducruet, C., H. Itoh, and O. Joly. 2015. "Ports and the Local Embedding of Commodity Flows." *Papers in Regional Science* 94 (3): 607–27.

Ducruet, C., F.Z. Mohamed-Chérif, and N. Cherfaoui. 2011. "Maghreb Port Cities in Transition: The Case of Tangier." *Portus Plus* 1 (1). http://retedigital.com/wp-content/themes/rete/pdfs/portus/Portus_21/maghreb_port_cities_in_transition_the_case_of_tangier.pdf.

Ferrari, C., F. Parola, and E. Morchio. 2006. "Southern European Ports and the Spatial Distribution of EDCs." *Maritime Economics and Logistics* 8 (1): 60–81.

Fujita, M., and T. Mori. 1996. "The Role of Ports in the Making of Major Cities: Self-Agglomeration and Hub-Effect." *Journal of Development Economics* 49 (1): 93–120.

Merk, O., and O. Bagis. 2013. "The Competitiveness of Global Port-Cities: The Case of Mersin." OECD Regional Development Working Paper 2013/01, Organisation for Economic Co-operation and Development, Paris.

Mohamed-Chérif, F. Z., and C. Ducruet. 2011. "Les ports et la façade maritime du Maghreb, entre intégration régionale et mondiale." *Mappemonde* 101. http://mappemonde-archive.mgm.fr/num29/articles/art11103.html.

Notteboom, T. E., and J. P. Rodrigue. 2005. "Port Regionalization: Towards a New Phase in Port Development." *Maritime Policy and Management* 32 (3): 297–313.

Slack, B., and E. Gouvernal. 2015. "Container Transshipment and Logistics in the Context of Urban Economic Development." *Growth and Change* 47 (3): 406–15.

Van den Berg, R., and P. W. De Langen. 2011. "Hinterland Strategies of Port Authorities: A Case Study of the Port of Barcelona." *Research in Transportation Economics* 33 (1): 6–14.

Appendix A
Guide to Port Locations

PORT	COUNTRY
Alexandria	Egypt, Arab Rep.
Algeciras	Spain, near Gibraltar
Algiers	Algeria
Ambarli	Turkey, near Istanbul
Ancona	Italy
Antalya	Turkey
Ashdod	Israel, near Tel Aviv
Bari	Italy
Benghazi	Libya
Bizerta	Tunisia
Bourgas	Bulgaria
Cagliari	Italy, island of Sardinia
Casablanca	Morocco
Castellon	Spain
Catania	Italy
Ceuta	Morocco
Chornomorsk	Ukraine
Civitavecchia	Italy
Constantza	Romania
Damietta	Egypt, Arab Rep., near Port Said
El Dekhiela	Egypt, Arab Rep., Alexandria
Evyap	Turkey
Fos	France, near Marseilles
Gemlik	Turkey
Gebze	Turkey, near Istanbul
Genoa	Italy
Ghazaouet	Algeria

(continued)

PORT	COUNTRY
Gioia Tauro	Italy, near Reggio Calabria
Haydarpasa	Turkey
Iraklion	Crete
Iskenderun	Turkey
Izmir	Turkey
Khoms	Libya
Koper	Slovenia
Lattakia	Turkey
La Spezia	Italy
Limassol	Cyprus
Livorno (Leghorn)	Italy
Malaga	Spain
Marsaxlokk	Malta
Marseilles	France
Mersin	Turkey
Misrata	Libya
Nemrut Bay	Turkey
Oran	Algeria
Piraeus	Greece, near Athens
Ploce	Croatia
Port Said	Egypt, Arab Rep., north end of the Suez Canal
Port Said East	Egypt, Arab Rep.
Port Said West	Egypt, Arab Rep.
Pozzallo	Italy
Radès	Tunisia, near Tunis
Sagunto	Spain
Salerno	Italy
Savona	Italy
Setubal	Portugal
Sines	Portugal
Sfax	Tunisia
Syros	Greece
Tanger Med	Morocco, near Tangier
Taranto	Italy
Tarragona	Spain
Tartous	Syrian Arab Republic
Thessaloniki	Greece
Trieste	Italy
Tuzla	Turkey
Valencia	Spain
Valletta	Malta
Varna	Bulgaria
Volos	Greece

Appendix B
Descriptions of 17 Major Mediterranean Ports

The sources for the data in the tables that follow are:

- Container volume: based on data provided by port authorities
- Principal role: defined as transshipment when more than 50 percent of the container cargo throughput consists of transshipment cargo
- Transshipment volume: provided by port authorities in most cases (for instance, Puertos del Estado for Spanish ports); in other cases call patterns provide a basis for defining ports as either a gateway or transshipment port
- Terminal productivity: calculated based on data from the *Journal of Commerce* (see chapter 2)
- Unique roll-on, roll-off destinations: calculations based on a database of such services that was collected firsthand
- Unique intermodal destinations: Calculations based on data from the Intermodal Links website (http://www.intermodallinks.com) and from port authority websites
- Presence of a free zone: determined based on an Internet search
- Presence of private specialized terminal operators: assessed through publicly available information on the terminal operating companies
- Institutional structure of the port authority/port development company: based on publicly available data (such as an annual report or a description of the corporate governance of the port authority/port development company).

ALEXANDRIA

The port of Alexandria, the largest gateway port in the Arab Republic of Egypt, is administered by the same port authority as the neighboring port of El Dekheila. Alexandria handles about 740,000 twenty-foot equivalent units (TEUs) per year, El Dekheila about 860,000. The terminal in Alexandria is operated by Hutchison Port Holdings. Alexandria and El Dekheila both serve the Cairo Metropolitan Area, mainly by road and with some barge services (table B.1).

TABLE B.1 **Performance indicators, Alexandria, 2016**

INDICATOR	PERFORMANCE
Container volume (TEUs)	750,000
Principal role	Gateway
Terminal productivity	30
Unique roll-on, roll-off destinations	29
Unique intermodal destinations	0
Presence of free zone	Yes
Private specialized terminal operators	Yes
Independent state-owned enterprise port development company	No

ALGECIRAS (SPAIN)

Algeciras is Spain's largest port in total volume (about 100 million tons) and the second largest container port in the Mediterranean (after Valencia), with a volume of 4.5 million twenty-foot equivalent units. The vast majority of traffic is transshipment. The largest terminal in Algeciras is APM Terminals, followed by Total Terminal International Algeciras, which was built and operated by Hanjin Group (which sold a 70 percent share to IBK Securities and Korea Investment Partners and was later sold to Hyundai Merchant Marine) and handled more than 900,000 twenty-foot equivalent units in 2016, down from around 1.2 million in 2012 and substantially below capacity of more than 1.8 million twenty-foot equivalent units. Algeciras has a rail connection to Madrid. The share of containers transported on rail is very low (less than 2 percent). There is no free zone in the port, but the Bay of Algeciras Logistics Area is a logistics platform of 300 hectares and has a rail terminal (table B.2).

TABLE B.2 **Performance indicators, Algeciras, 2016**

INDICATOR	PERFORMANCE
Container volume (TEUs)	4,515,768
Principal role	Transshipment
Terminal productivity	49
Unique roll-on, roll-off destinations	2
Unique intermodal destinations	1
Presence of free zone	No
Private specialized terminal operators	Yes
Independent state-owned enterprise port development company	No

ALGIERS

The port of Algiers is located in the northwestern part of the Bay of Algiers and handles 33 percent of Algeria's foreign trade. Its hinterland covers the center, east center, and west center of Algeria. The port and its hinterland are connected by rail (the rail network is mainly in the north). One container terminal, covering an area of more than 30 hectares, is run by Entreprise Portuaire d'Alger and managed by DP World under a 30-year concession that began in 2009. The container terminal has two berths: one 435 meters in length and one 337 meters in length.

Multipurpose berths of more than 500 meters are also used for containers when needed. There are several feeder services from Spain (Barcelona and Valencia) and France (Marseilles). In 2015 container throughput was 852,000 twenty-foot equivalent units, and total throughput was around 16 million tons. There is no free zone (table B.3).

TABLE B.3 **Performance indicators, Algiers, 2016**

INDICATOR	PERFORMANCE
Container volume (TEUs)	851,743[a]
Principal role	Gateway
Terminal productivity	13
Unique roll-on, roll-off destinations	1
Unique intermodal destinations	0
Presence of free zone	No
Private specialized terminal operators	Yes
Independent state-owned enterprise port development company	No

a. Data are for 2015.

AMBARLI (TURKEY)

During the establishment stage of Ambarli port in the 1990s, several companies wanted to operate there. Because the Turkish Ministry of Transport and public institutions wanted one integrated partner, a port development partnership of six terminal operators and one pilotage company (called ATLAS) was established. Three operators handle containers, the largest of which is Marport, part of a large Turkish transport and logistics group (Arkas). The rail connections are poorly developed, however, and cargo from continental Europe is sometimes taken by rail to another port, such as Constantza (Romania) or Trieste (Italy) and shipped by container or roll-on, roll-off vessel to Ambarli. There is a free zone close to Ambarli (table B.4).

TABLE B.4 **Performance indicators, Ambarli, 2016**

INDICATOR	PERFORMANCE
Container volume (TEUs)	3,200,000
Principal role	Transshipment
Terminal productivity	30
Unique roll-on, roll-off destinations	1
Unique intermodal destinations	— (probably 0)
Presence of free zone	Yes (Istanbul)
Private specialized terminal operators	Yes
Independent state-owned enterprise port development company	Yes

Note: — = not available.

BENGHAZI (LIBYA)

The port of Benghazi (and its container terminal) is owned and run by the state-owned Ports Company. Containers are handled alongside the general berth in a multipurpose terminal. Container throughput in 2012 was 156,000 twenty-foot equivalent units. There is no railway connection (ones previously developed have fallen into disrepair). There is no free zone (Libya's only free trade zone in is in Misrata port) (table B.5).

TABLE B.5 **Performance indicators, Benghazi, 2016**

INDICATOR	PERFORMANCE
Container volume (TEUs)	156,275[a]
Principal role	Gateway
Terminal productivity	20[b]
Unique roll-on, roll-off destinations	7
Unique intermodal destinations	0
Presence of free zone	No
Private specialized terminal operators	No
Independent state-owned enterprise port development company	No

a. Data are for 2012.
b. Data are for 2014.

CASABLANCA

The port of Casablanca is Morocco's main gateway port, serving the Casablanca metropolitan region and most of central Morocco. Casablanca has two container terminals, both with private operators: Marsa Maroc, the largest operator in Morocco, and Somaport, an independent terminal operator. Casablanca does not have regular container train services. It is also an important roll-on, roll-off port, with destinations in Europe, North Africa, and West Africa (table B.6).

TABLE B.6 **Performance indicators, Casablanca, 2016**

INDICATOR	PERFORMANCE
Container volume (TEUs)	951,000[a]
Principal role	Gateway
Terminal productivity	14[b]
Unique roll-on, roll-off destinations	45
Unique intermodal destinations	0
Presence of free zone	No
Private specialized terminal operators	Yes
Independent state-owned enterprise port development company	No

a. Data are for 2016.
b. Data are for 2015.

GENOA

The port of Genoa is Italy's largest gateway port, serving northern Italy as well as Central Europe. There are two container terminals. The largest is operated by PSA, the Singapore-based global terminal operator, and the other is operated by SECH Terminal Contenitori Porto di Genova. Genoa has regular frequent direct rail connections to four inland rail terminals. Genoa is also a large roll-on, roll-off port, with destinations in Europe as well as North Africa (table B.7).

TABLE B.7 **Performance indicators, Genoa, 2016**

INDICATOR	PERFORMANCE
Container volume (TEUs)	2,243,000[a]
Principal role	Gateway
Terminal productivity	39[a]
Unique roll-on, roll-off destinations	23
Unique intermodal destinations	4
Presence of free zone	No
Private specialized terminal operators	Yes
Independent state-owned enterprise port development company	No

a. Data are for 2015.

GIOIA TAURO (ITALY)

The port of Gioia Tauro is the largest port in Italy by container volume. It has one container terminal operated by Medcenter container terminal under a concession. The terminal has an area of 1.6 million square meters and total quay length of 3,400 meters. Throughput in 2015 was close to 3 million twenty-foot equivalent units (total handling capacity is 4.2 million) (table B.8).

TABLE B.8 **Performance indicators, Gioia Tauro, 2016**

INDICATOR	PERFORMANCE
Container volume (TEUs)	2,969,802[a]
Principal role	Transshipment
Terminal productivity	26
Unique roll-on, roll-off destinations	0
Unique intermodal destinations	1
Presence of free zone	No
Private specialized terminal operators	Yes
Independent state-owned enterprise port development company	No

a. Data are for 2015.

MARSAXLOKK (MALTA)

The Port Authority of Marsaxlokk was established in 1988 to run the container terminals in the port. In late 2004 the government of Malta awarded CMA CGM a 30-year concession to operate and develop Malta Freeport Terminals. In 2008 it granted CMA CGM an extension of the concession to 65 years. There are two container terminals, where more than 3 million twenty-foot equivalent units were handled in 2015 (more than 90 percent of it transshipment). Malta Freeport has a free trade zone (table B.9).

TABLE B.9 **Performance indicators, Marsaxlokk, 2016**

INDICATOR	PERFORMANCE
Container volume (TEUs)	3,060,000[a]
Principal role	Transshipment
Terminal productivity	48
Unique roll-on, roll-off destinations	0
Unique intermodal destinations	0
Presence of free zone	Yes
Private specialized terminal operators	Yes
Independent state-owned enterprise port development company	Yes

a. Data are for 2015.

MARSEILLES

The port of Marseilles has two harbors: the eastern harbor (in the city) and the western harbor in Fos (around 50 kilometers to the west of the city). The port has three container terminals: one in the eastern harbor and two in the western harbor. The container terminal in the eastern harbor, known as the Mediterranean Europe terminal, is operated under concession by Intramar. The container terminals in Fos, known as Fos 2xl terminals, are operated under concession by Eurofos and Seayard. The terminal run by Eurofos is called Terminal de Méditerranée and is managed by China Merchant, CMA CGM, and DP World, and the terminal run by Seayard is managed by AMP Terminals, COSCO, Mediterranean Shipping Company, and Terminal Investment Limited. The terminals handled 1.2 million twenty-foot equivalent units in 2015. The rail network offers services for all types of cargo—dry and reefer (refrigerated) containers, breakbulk, and liquid and solid bulk—and links the port to other French cities and northern European ports. There is no free trade zone (table B.10).

TABLE B.10 **Performance indicators, Marseilles, 2016**

INDICATOR	PERFORMANCE
Container volume (TEUs)	1,223,071[a]
Principal role	Gateway
Terminal productivity	51
Unique roll-on, roll-off destinations	7
Unique intermodal destinations	21 (rail and inland shipping)
Presence of free zone	No
Private specialized terminal operators	Yes
Independent state-owned enterprise port development company	No

a. Data are for 2015.

MERSIN (TURKEY)

The Turkish port of Mersin has one container terminal run by Mersin International Port Management Inc., which was established in 2007 as a partnership between Akfen Holding and PSA International for 36 years.

Total container throughput in 2015 was close to 1.5 million twenty-foot equivalent units. There is a railway connection between the container terminal and its hinterlands. Mersin port has a free trade zone.

TABLE B.11 **Performance indicators, Mersin, 2016**

INDICATOR	PERFORMANCE
Container volume (TEUs)	1,470,000
Principal role	Gateway
Terminal productivity	45
Unique roll-on, roll-off destinations	7
Unique intermodal destinations	—
Presence of free zone	Yes
Private specialized terminal operators	Yes
Independent state-owned enterprise port development company	Yes

Note: — = not available.

PIRAEUS

The Greek port of Piraeus has two terminals handling containers: Terminal I (Pier I) and Terminal II (Pier II and Pier III). Terminal I, with a capacity of 1 million twenty-foot equivalent units, is operated by the Piraeus Port Authority (which has been majority owned by China COSCO Shipping Group since August 2016). Terminal II is run by COSCO Pacific under a 35-year concession signed in 2008. The agreement between Piraeus Port Authority and COSCO allowed investment not only in new piers, but also in a rail link between the port's terminals and the national rail system. Total container throughput in 2015 was 3.3 million twenty-foot equivalent units. Piraeus port has a free trade zone.

TABLE B.12 **Performance indicators, Piraeus, 2016**

INDICATOR	PERFORMANCE
Container volume (TEUs)	3,287,000[a]
Principal role	Transshipment
Terminal productivity	48
Unique roll-on, roll-off destinations	22
Unique intermodal destinations	1
Presence of free zone	Yes
Private specialized terminal operators	Yes
Independent state-owned enterprise port development company	Yes

a. Data are for 2015.

PORT SAID (EGYPT)

Port Said has two container terminals. One is run by Suez Canal Container Terminal (under a 2004 agreement), and the other is run by Port Said Container & Cargo Handling Co. The Suez Canal Container Terminal shareholders are APM Terminals (55 percent), COSCO Pacific (20 percent),

Suez Canal Authority & Affiliates (10 percent), the Egyptian private sector (10 percent), and the National Bank of Egypt (5 percent). Port Said Container & Cargo Handling Co. is a joint-stock Egyptian company affiliated with the holding company for Maritime & Land Transport. Port Said has a free trade zone.

TABLE B.13 **Performance indicators, Port Said, 2016**

INDICATOR	PERFORMANCE
Container volume (TEUs)	3,400,000[a]
Principal role	Transshipment
Terminal productivity	37
Unique roll-on, roll-off destinations	0
Unique intermodal destinations	0
Presence of free zone	Yes
Private specialized terminal operators	Yes
Independent state-owned enterprise port development company	No

a. Data are for 2014.

RADÈS (TUNISIA)

The port of Radès has one container terminal run by the state-owned company, Office de la Marine Marchande et de Ports. The port conveys 76 percent of Tunisia's container traffic. In 2012 container throughput was 1.8 million twenty-foot equivalent units. There is a rail link between the port and the hinterland. There are two free trade zones in Tunis (table B.14).

TABLE B.14 **Performance indicators, Radès, 2016**

INDICATOR	PERFORMANCE
Container volume (TEUs)[a]	1,800,000
Principal role	Gateway
Terminal productivity	6
Unique roll-on, roll-off destinations	5
Unique intermodal destinations	—
Presence of free zone	Yes, near Radès, in Tunis
Private specialized terminal operators	No
Independent state-owned enterprise port development company	Yes[b]

Note: — = is not available.
a. Data are for 2012.
b. The Merchant Marine and Ports Authority has a predominantly political supervisory board.

SINES (PORTUGAL)

The Sines Container Terminal, called Terminal XXI, started operations in 2004 under a 30-year public service concession to PSA Sines, a wholly owned subsidiary of the global terminal operator PSA. The port itself is relatively modern: construction began in 1973 and became officially operational in 1978. Apart from containers, the port handles bulk liquids. The port has rail connections to the

Portuguese hinterland but handles mainly transshipment cargo. Traffic has grown quickly in recent years, to 1.3 million twenty-foot equivalent units in 2015. There is a modest logistics park close to the port (table B.15).

TABLE B.15 **Performance indicators, Sines, 2016**

INDICATOR	PERFORMANCE
Container volume (twenty-foot equivalent units)	1,332,000[a]
Principal role	Transshipment
Terminal productivity	—
Unique roll-on, roll-off destinations	0
Unique intermodal destinations	3
Presence of free zone	No
Private specialized terminal operators	Yes
Independent state-owned enterprise port development company	Yes[b]

Note: — = is not available.
a. Data are for 2015.
b. The Sines port authority has a predominantly political supervisory board.

TANGER MED (MOROCCO)

Tanger Med 1 has two container terminals. The first started operations in 2007, the second in 2008. The first container terminal is operated under a 30-year concession, granted in 2005 to APM Terminals Tangier, a subsidiary of APM Terminals Group. The second container terminal is also operated under a 30-year concession, granted in 2006 to a consortium of Contship Italia (Europe's leading port operator), Eurogate Tanger, and two shipping companies (CMA CGM and MSC). After Tanger Med's success in attracting terminal operators and shipping lines, Tanger Med 2 was developed, starting in 2010 (it is not yet operational). Tanger Med 2 will have two container terminals: one operated by Marsa Morocco, and the other by APM Terminals. Tanger Med has four export-oriented free trade zones. Tangier has had a rail terminal for containers since 2009, managed by l'Office National des Chemins de Fer, the Moroccan rail operator. The terminal offers a network of connections in Morocco, including to the Dry Port in Casablanca (MITA) (table B.16).

TABLE B.16 **Performance indicators, Tanger Med, 2016**

INDICATOR	PERFORMANCE
Container volume (twenty-foot equivalent units)	2,971,336
Principal role	Transshipment
Terminal productivity	47
Unique roll-on, roll-off destinations	3
Unique intermodal destinations	n.a.
Presence of free zone	Yes (four)
Private specialized terminal operators	Yes
Independent state-owned enterprise port development company	Yes[a]

Note: n.a. = not applicable.
a. The Tanger Med Port Authority has a predominantly political supervisory board.

VALENCIA (SPAIN)

The Spanish port of Valencia has three container terminals, called Terminal Pública de Contenedores (run by Noatum Container Terminal Valencia), MSC Terminal Valencia (run by MSC Terminal Valencia), and APM Terminals Valencia (run by APM Terminals). These three terminals are operated under concessions that will end around 2030. In 2016 total container throughput was 4.72 million twenty-foot equivalent units. Four rail companies operate at the port: Logitren Ferroviaria, Renfe Mercancías, SISCA Rail Transport, and TCV Railway Transport. The port has no free trade zone (table B.17).

TABLE B.17 **Performance indicators, Valencia, 2016**

INDICATOR	PERFORMANCE
Container volume (TEUs)	4,722,000
Principal role	Transshipment
Terminal productivity	37
Unique roll-on, roll-off destinations	33
Unique intermodal destinations	5
Presence of free zone	No
Private specialized terminal operators	Yes
Independent state-owned enterprise port development company	No

Glossary

An asterisk indicates that the definition is drawn from Rodrigue, J.-P., C. Comtois, and B. Slack, 2017, *The Geography of Transport Systems,* 4th ed., New York: Routledge.

alliance. A global group of shipping companies that cooperate to offer more comprehensive coverage of trade route than individual members can.

centrality. A network concept that captures how central the topological position of a node of network is with respect to all other nodes of the network. In the context of ports and shipping networks, it relates to the topological accessibility of a port with regard to other ports. There are several concepts of centrality: degree centrality refers to the number of links to other ports, betweenness centrality refers to the number of shortest paths connecting the port, eigenvalue centrality refers to the probability that a random walk on the network hits a port, and closeness centrality is the average number of steps to reach the port from elsewhere.

direct/adjacent call. A vessel movement between two ports without any intermediary stops—that is, with a single voyage between them.

diversion distance. The distance in nautical miles to or from the trunk line.

feeder. Short-sea shipping service that connects at least two ports in order for the freight (generally containers) to be consolidated or redistributed to or from a deep-sea service in one of the ports. By extension, this concept may be used for inland transport services and air transportation.*

foreland. The maritime space with which a port performs commercial relationships. It includes overseas customers with which the port undertakes commercial exchanges.*

gateway. A location offering accessibility to a large system of circulation of freight, passengers, or information. Gateways reap the advantage of a favorable physical location such as a highway junction or confluence of rivers and seaboards and accumulate substantial transport infrastructure such as terminals and their links. A gateway generally commands the entrance to or the exit from its catchment area. In other words, it is a pivotal point for the entrance and exit of merchandise in a region, country, or continent. Gateways tend to be locations where intermodal transfers are performed.*

generalized transport costs. Out-of-pocket costs for transport and additional costs, of which inventory costs are generally the most important.

hinterland. The land space over which a transport terminal, such as a port, sells its services and interacts with clients. It accounts for the regional market share that a terminal has relative to a set of other terminals servicing the same region. It regroups all the customers directly bounded to the terminal. The terminal, depending on its nature, serves as a place of convergence for the traffic coming by road, rail, or sea or fluvial feeders.*

hub. The central point for collecting, sorting, transshipping, and distributing goods and passengers for a particular area. The concept comes from a term used in air transport for passengers as well as freight. It describes collection and distribution through a single point such as the hub-and-spoke and interlining concepts. Hubs tend to be transmodal (transfers within the same mode) locations.*

interlining. Transshipment activity in which mother vessels exchange containers at certain hub ports at the intersection of main trunk lines such as east–west and north–south.

intermodal transport. The movement of goods in the same loading unit or road vehicle using two or more modes of transport that do not handle the goods when modes are changed. Intermodal transport enables cargo to be consolidated into economically large units (containers, bulk grain railcars, and the like) optimized for specialized intermodal handling equipment that effects high-speed cargo transfer between ships, barges, railcars, and truck chassis using a minimum of labor to increase logistic flexibility, reduce consignment delivery times, and minimize operating costs.*

landlord port model. A model in which port functions are unbundled between a regulator (port authority) and commercial operations. Operators can be private, state-owned, or mixed enterprises.

liner. A vessel that operates along a defined route on a fixed schedule, usually hauling general cargo (rather than bulk cargo).*

mode. The physical way a movement is performed (type of transportation).*

mother vessel. A larger vessel that makes direct calls at larger hub or gateway ports.

node. A terminal point or an intersection point of a graph. It is the abstraction of a location such as a city, an administrative division, a road intersection, or a transport terminal (stations, terminuses, harbors, and airports).*

Panamax. A maritime standard corresponding to about 65,000 deadweight tons or 4,000 twenty-foot equivalent units. A Panamax ship's dimensions allow it to pass through the Panama Canal: maximum length 295 meters, maximum beam overall 32.25 meters, and maximum draught 13.50 meters. Post-Panamax refers to ships that exceed the Panamax standard. Super Post-Panamax or Post-Panamax Plus refers to the largest of those ships, which usually exceed 8,000 twenty-foot equivalent units.*

pendulum service. A set of sequential port calls along a maritime range, often including transoceanic service from ports in another range and structured as a continuous loop. Pendulum service is used almost exclusively for container transportation to service a market by balancing the number of port calls and the frequency of service.*

roll-on, roll-off. Transportation of commercial vehicles, articulated ensembles, or nonmotorized trailers on specialized ships, such as ferries.

short-sea shipping. Commercial waterborne transportation that does not transit an ocean. It is an alternative form of commercial transportation that uses inland and coastal waterways to move commercial freight from major domestic ports to its destination.*

transshipment port. A port whose primary business is transshipment of containers between large vessels on trunk lines and smaller vessels on feeder lines. Transshipment ports are typically hubs.

transshipment. The transfer of goods (containers) from one carrier to another or from one mode to another.*

trunk line. The route realized by the regular voyages of mother vessels. A trunk line may overlap the various pendulum or round-the-world services of major ocean carriers where they deploy their largest vessels.

twenty-foot equivalent unit. A standard unit based on an International Organization for Standardization container that is 20 feet (6.10 meters) long, used as a statistical measure of traffic flows or capacities.*

vulnerability. Situation in which a port depends heavily on another port for traffic flows. Ducruet (2008) measures vulnerability using as hub dependence index that is the share of a port's largest flow link in the port's total vessel traffic (usually in twenty-foot equivalent units).

www.ingramcontent.com/pod-product-compliance
Lightning Source LLC
Chambersburg PA
CBHW081422230426

43668CB00016B/2320